Hyperactive Happiness

Turning Challenges Into Triumphs While Parenting Kids With ADHD

Alexis Carter

Other Books by Alexis Carter:

The Doormat Series of Self-Help Books and Workbooks

Stop Being a Doormat and Learn to Love Yourself

Ditching the Doormat

The Doormat Dater

Leave That Junk Behind- A Self-Esteem Workbook for Adults

You've Got This Girl- A Self-Esteem Workbook for Girls

Hyperactive Happiness

Table of Contents

Introduction

Asking for help with shame says: 'You have power over me.' Asking with condescension says: 'I have the power over you.' But asking for help with gratitude says: 'We have the power to help each other.'
—Amanda Palmer

I started noticing signs that my twins have Attention Deficit Hyperactivity Disorder (ADHD) around the time they turned seven years old. They had just started kindergarten then, and there was something about being in a new environment that brought their symptoms to the surface. Before they attended school, I had already noticed that they were very active kids, especially when they were playing with each other, although I didn't think they were *hyper*active. I believed their behavior was normal because, as toddlers, they were going through developmental stages in their lives.

It was actually their kindergarten teacher (let's call her Mrs. Hawthorne) who first brought my children's behavioral issues to my attention. Mrs. Hawthorne had more than fifteen years of experience in early childhood education, so if anyone was an expert on the normal markers of growth and development, it would be her. Anyway, she told me that the twins would often leave their seats when they were not supposed to, talk to each other loudly during class, and interrupt their friends during activities. They were also easily distracted and had short attention spans. With her expertise, she determined that these behaviors, based on their extent and frequency, warranted further examination.

So I started observing my twins at home to see if the behavioral issues Mrs. Hawthorne had pointed out would manifest outside of school, too. Sure enough, I began noticing other signs that there might be a problem needing my attention. For instance, I found myself having to give instructions repeatedly before my twins acknowledged and followed them. They would fidget with their hands or tap their feet constantly whenever we sat in the living room to watch TV. They were also easily frustrated whenever I refused to give them what they wanted, like snacks before dinner or ice cream on a cold day, and their frustrations would often turn into outbursts or tantrums that were difficult to bring under control.

These were just some examples of the issues I noticed after meeting with Mrs. Hawthorne. With her encouragement, I brought my twins to a child psychologist for an assessment, where they were formally diagnosed with ADHD before they turned eight years old.

After my twins were diagnosed, I did my best to educate myself on ADHD, its symptoms, and its impact on their lives. I read books and consulted with the child psychologist to see what kind of support I could offer my children. I also enlisted the help of Mrs. Hawthorne so I could be confident that they were receiving the right care at school, too. My children are older now, and they have been following a routine that allows them to effectively manage their ADHD symptoms.

If you're a working parent like myself, you know how challenging it is to balance work and childcare. I'm also a single parent, so I often feel guilty about not being able to spend more time with my twins. Without Mrs. Hawthorne's help, I don't think I would have noticed that my children had behavioral issues that needed to be addressed. I would have continued to believe that their ADHD symptoms were a normal part of their growth. I wouldn't have known that they have a neurodevelopmental disorder until their symptoms had worsened.

Because of Mrs. Hawthorne's expert advice, I was able to bring my children to a psychologist for an assessment sooner rather than later. Therefore, I was able to implement a management and treatment strategy that prevented worse issues from occurring and, at the same time, empowered my children to navigate their diagnosis as they grew up.

Mrs. Hawthorne is actually one of my inspirations behind writing this book: Just like she helped me years ago, I want to pay it forward and provide advice and assistance to other parents who may be struggling with the same issues while raising kids with ADHD.

This book contains practical advice and actionable steps that you can take to help your children effectively manage their ADHD symptoms. I learned these tips after years of educating myself about this neurodevelopmental disorder and seeking the advice of specialists like special education teachers, child psychologists, and other parents whose children have the same condition. This is a culmination of my experience as a parent of twins with ADHD, and I am proud to say that I wouldn't have been able to write this book without guidance from others.

Aside from providing you with helpful tips to effectively manage your children's ADHD symptoms, I also included a chapter specifically for parents so you can look after yourself while navigating your children's diagnosis. We will talk about common issues that parents of kids with ADHD face and how you can overcome them. I'm a firm believer that parents won't be able to provide the best care to their children if they're not taking care of themselves. In other words, self-care is an important part of our role as parents, so you should never neglect your own needs.

With all of this said, I am excited to embark on this journey with you! Aside from helping you better understand ADHD and its impact on our children, I want this book to be a safe and positive space for parents like you to feel seen, heard, and validated. There will be sections at the end of each chapter where you can review key learnings, as well as exercises where you can test your understanding and practice self-reflection. Let me help you navigate your children's diagnosis, so you can, in turn, help them navigate their reality with boundless hope, curiosity, and positivity. We are all in this together.

Chapter 1:

Understanding ADHD

You have to acknowledge a problem exists before you can actually go about finding a solution.
–Demi Moore

Often, as parents, we fall victim to our own arrogant belief that we always know what is best for our children. I have seen many parents make the mistake of trying to find solutions to their children's less-than-desirable behaviors without actually understanding the root cause of the problem. When these symptoms start to show up, many parents will attempt to "fix" their children with solutions unbefitting their special needs, which can result in bigger and more complicated issues as they grow up.

Not only that, children with ADHD are often stereotyped as rowdy, lazy, defiant, noisy, and bad at school, among many other things, because their neurodivergent behaviors are compared to those of their neurotypical peers. This comparison leads some adults to believe that one type of kid is "good" while the other is "bad"—a gross oversimplification of an issue as complicated as ADHD, which is a neurodevelopmental disorder that can affect every facet of a child's life.

Just like the actress Demi Moore once said, we can't find solutions if we don't acknowledge what the problem actually is. And for us to acknowledge the real problem behind our children's behavioral issues, we must first understand the disorder that inspires them.

In this chapter, we will discuss what ADHD is in an attempt to better understand it as a neurodevelopmental disorder. In particular, we will answer two central questions that will lay the foundation for our discussion throughout this book. First, what is ADHD? Second, what are its symptoms and how do they affect our children's lives?

What Is ADHD?

According to the World Health Organization (WHO, 2019), Attention Deficit Hyperactivity Disorder (ADHD) is a neurodevelopmental disorder that affects about five to eight percent of children. Its main characteristics include inattentiveness, hyperactivity, and impulsivity, which we will discuss further in the next subchapter.

Individuals with ADHD have deficiencies in neurotransmitters, specifically dopamine and norepinephrine, which are related to important executive functions such as memory, attention, and learning. They are also related to self-control and reward (Cleveland Clinic, 2022; Villines, 2023). Aside from dopamine and norepinephrine, evidence also shows a connection between ADHD and "dysfunction in serotonin (5-hydroxytryptamine, acetylcholine, opioid, and glutamate pathways," which are responsible for "executive function, working memory, emotional regulation, and reward processing" (Faraone, 2018). These deficiencies may result in executive dysfunction, chronic procrastination, and risky behaviors, among other disruptive outcomes, if symptoms are not managed properly.

There is still not enough data to determine the exact cause of ADHD, although there is some evidence that this disorder is genetic. If one or both parents have ADHD, then their child is more likely to also be born with this disorder. Other possible causes include childhood trauma, premature birth, and brain injury. It may also be a result of alcohol and tobacco use by the mother during pregnancy, as well as exposure to environmental risks, like high levels of lead (Centers for Disease Control and Prevention [CDC], 2022a; National Health Service [NHS], 2021a; WHO, 2019).

ADHD was widely believed to be a childhood disorder, but more recent studies show that symptoms can persist into adulthood (CDC, 2022a; NHS, 2021b). Therefore, it is important to find an effective symptom management strategy as early as possible if more complicated issues are to be avoided in the future.

ADHD also falls under the umbrella of neurodiversity, which includes other neurodevelopmental disorders like Autism Spectrum Disorder (ASD), Tourette's Syndrome, and Obsessive-Compulsive Disorder (OCD), as well as learning disabilities like dyslexia (Baumer & Frueh, 2021; "Neurodivergent," 2017).

Admittedly, neurodiversity is a subject I didn't know much about before my twins were diagnosed with ADHD. However, after learning more about it, I'm glad that I looked into it because it offered me a new perspective that empowered me as a parent of neurodivergent kids. Before we discuss what the common symptoms of ADHD are, I want us to first talk about ADHD from the lens of neurodiversity. I also want to debunk some misconceptions many people have about this disorder.

Neurodiversity

Every human being has their own set of characteristics and abilities that make them different from everyone else. However, our society has labeled certain characteristics and abilities as "normal" or good"—in turn, those who deviate from these categories are considered "bad" and may even face discrimination simply because they are different.

For example, non-neurotypical individuals, i.e. those who have neurodevelopmental disorders like ADHD and ASD, have traits that are considered "bad" by standards of neurotypicality—executive dysfunction is reduced to laziness, time blindness is reduced to tardiness, and emotion dysregulation is reduced to misbehavior. These categorizations often result in the othering of non-neurotypical individuals or neurodivergents, also called NNTs or NDs, in society.

This othering takes many shapes and forms. For instance, many studies have shown that non-neurotypical children are more prone to bullying compared to their neurotypical peers (Bustinza, et al., 2022; Fogler, 2020; Junttila, et al., 2023; Murray et al., 2020; Park et al., 2020). School-aged NNTs are bullied not only by their peers but also by adults and authority figures such as coaches and teachers. They experience bullying in school and online. With the prevalence of social media in our daily lives, children with neurodevelopmental disorders become targets of increasing cyberbullying (ADDitude Editors, 2023a; National Children's Bureau, 2023).

Judy Singer, an Australian sociologist, was the first person to use the term "neurodiversity" in 1998, and it has since been used to define the social movement that aims to increase the visibility and inclusion of people with neurodevelopmental disorders in society (Baumer & Frueh, 2021; Lutz, 2023; Miller, 2023a; "Neurodivergent," 2022). Through the lens of neurodiversity, human brains are either neurotypical or neurodivergent, but there is not one that is "normal" or "abnormal" simply because "there's no single definition of 'normal' for how the human brain works" ("Neurodivergent," 2022).

To further explore this definition, let's look at three different stories from blind individuals. The first one is Sara Minkara, the founder of Empowerment Through Integration (ETI), a non-profit organization whose goal is to create a more inclusive society for people with disabilities (Empowerment Through Integration, n.d.). At seven years old, macular degeneration caused Sara to lose her eyesight, but she doesn't think her blindness is a limitation. In an interview, she said, "I think the biggest obstacle that surrounds our disabilities is the social construct around us. … When you eliminate the stigma, to be honest, then dealing with your disability is not that big a thing" (Ahmad, 2019).

Gertrude Oforiwa Fefoame, the chairperson of the United Nations Committee on the Rights of Persons with Disabilities (UNCRPD), said something similar in an interview. According to her, "it is not the presence of the impairment, but it is the social and attitudinal barriers that are hindering our performance" (Daniel, 2023).

I've also spoken to a visually impaired person who doesn't consider her blindness a disability. My family used to live close to a person who was born blind. Let's call her Amanda. When my twins were diagnosed with ADHD, I decided to pay her a visit because I learned through research that ADHD is classified as a disability under the *Americans With Disabilities Act* (Yellin, 2023). Back then, I was worried that my children would experience hardships that I couldn't prepare them for because of their diagnosis.

Amanda was kind enough to lend me an ear when I needed someone to listen to my concerns. When I asked her how her disability affected her daily life, she smiled and said, "Being blind is all I've ever known. This is normal to me, so I don't really see it as a disability, no pun intended. This is just who I am. It's the rest of the world that tells me I'm disabled just because I'm different."

Her answer was shocking because, as someone with sight, I've always thought of blindness as a disability. I can't imagine waking up one day and not being able to see the world around me. To never be able to watch my favorite movies again, to never be able to see the beautiful colors of the sunset, and to never be able to witness my children growing up before my eyes—I would be horrified if these things were to happen suddenly!

But Amanda, who was born blind, isn't upset over something she never had. Instead of feeling downtrodden about what she doesn't have, she's extremely grateful for the things she *does* have. She loves cooking and singing, both of which don't need a sense of sight to be done well. Moreover, she has her own way of "seeing" the world around her, which is different from how I see the world, yet is not inferior or lesser-than.

Sara, Gertrude, and Amanda are all individuals with a physical disability, and I think their attitude toward their blindness can also be applied to mental disabilities and neurodevelopmental disorders like ADHD and ASD. This world is designed to cater to neurotypicals. Our society favors neurotypicals. Neurotypicals take for granted the privileges and advantages that are not available to neurodivergents—I can say this with certainty because *I* am neurotypical. I have seen the discrimination that neurodivergent people face in society and have compared it to my own experiences. With all of this said, we need to keep in mind that it is not our children's neurodivergence but the current social norms surrounding their disorders and disabilities that hinder them from reaching their full potential.

To be honest, I am still continuously learning to shift my perspective to a more positive direction so that I don't become the source of stigma surrounding their disorder. Of course, as a parent, I still can't help but worry about the challenges they will face as they grow up.

However, I've come to realize that the most important thing for me, as their parent, is to foster an environment where ADHD doesn't become my children's limit. If we can provide a supportive and positive space for our children, then they will grow up thinking that their neurodivergence is not a hindrance to life but simply a normal part of it—that their neurodivergence makes them different, yes, but it doesn't make them any less than others.

Society at large may not change how it views neurodiversity by tomorrow, but we can start that change at our homes today. We should be our children's biggest advocates so that they can face the world as confident individuals who are not afraid of or apologetic about being their authentic selves.

Misconceptions

Aside from the social stigma that neurodivergent people face on a daily basis, there are also misconceptions surrounding ADHD that further influence negative perceptions toward affected individuals. In this section, let's talk about five of the most common misconceptions that we often hear about this disorder and set the record straight. What is the truth about ADHD?

1. ADHD Is Not a Disability

As I mentioned earlier, ADHD is legally considered a disability under the Americans With Disabilities Act (ADA), which was enacted in 1990 and amended in 2008. The ADA was passed for people with physical and mental impairments, so ADHD *is* a disability, and individuals with this condition have certain protections against discrimination as stated in the law (Yellin, 2023).

According to the *Americans With Disabilities Act of 1990*, the term "disability" pertains to "a physical or mental impairment that substantially limits one or more major life activities," including but not limited to "caring for oneself, performing manual tasks, seeing, hearing, eating, sleeping, walking, standing, lifting, bending, speaking, breathing, learning, reading, concentrating, thinking, communicating, and working."

When we talked about neurodiversity in the previous section, I told the story of three individuals who didn't view their blindness as a disability, which I think should inspire us to shift our perspective toward our children's diagnosis. I also encouraged you to foster an environment where ADHD doesn't limit your children's ability to reach their full potential. At the same time, we recognized that other people's perception of ADHD and other neurodevelopmental disorders will not change overnight. In fact, I think it will take society a long time to realize and accept that certain conditions do not make one lesser than others but simply different.

Because we can't change the world quickly enough for our children to live in a society that doesn't judge them for their neurodevelopmental disorder, it is important to remember that ADHD is legally recognized as a disability in this country and is therefore protected against discrimination by law. You should read up on the Americans With Disabilities Act and equip yourself with its provisions so you know your children's rights and can properly and legally protect them should the need arise.

If you live outside of the United States, you should look into what your legal system says about neurodevelopmental disorders and other mental health impairments. Different countries have different legislations and protections for disabilities under their respective laws, so I highly recommend that you do further research about this topic to be prepared should any unfortunate events occur.

2. ADHD Affects More Boys Than Girls

According to the CDC (2022b), 13% of boys and 6% of girls in the United States have ADHD. While the statement above is statistically correct, the reality is more nuanced than what the numbers show us.

See, there are three types of ADHD that affected individuals can fall into depending on their symptoms: the predominantly inattentive type, the predominantly hyperactive/impulsive type, and the combined type. We will discuss each of these types in more detail in the next subchapter.

Studies have shown that girls with ADHD are more the inattentive type, while boys with ADHD are more the hyperactive/impulsive type (Skogli et al., 2013; Slobodin & Davidovitch, 2019; Tee-Melegrito, 2022). Symptoms of the inattentive type are more internalized, while those of the hyperactive/impulsive type are more externalized. Therefore, the latter is more observable, resulting in boys being more likely to receive a diagnosis than girls. The internalized symptoms of the inattentive type lead many girls to go undiagnosed, be misdiagnosed, or be diagnosed later in life.

There is also evidence that girls remain undiagnosed "because they often display more symptoms of anxiety" and, as a result, are only treated for "anxiety or depression without evaluating for ADHD." In adolescence, hormonal changes may also affect how and which symptoms manifest, which further complicates or delays a girl's diagnosis (Children and Adults with Attention-Deficit/Hyperactivity Disorder [CHADD], 2021).

Another explanation as to why boys are more often diagnosed with ADHD is found in the existing literature. Most early studies around ADHD were conducted on boys, so there has been more emphasis on their symptoms (Kingsley & Connolly, 2023). It is only in recent years that more researchers are looking into the gender differences of ADHD and its symptoms. Thanks to these new studies, we are now able to determine that girls are more inattentive and are therefore less likely to show the stereotypical characteristics and behaviors that hint at this neurodevelopmental disorder. With this information, parents and teachers have more information on key markers of ADHD in girls so that they can support all children.

Despite the possible underdiagnosis of girls with ADHD, their symptoms still lead to challenges in school, at home, and in social settings. Moreover, late diagnosis of ADHD can have a lasting impact on an individual, such as chronic stress, anxiety, and low self-esteem, as they enter their adolescence and adulthood (Fairbank, 2023; Kingsley & Connolly, 2023). It can also "bring up some complicated emotions, whether it's grief over lost opportunities, relief at finally understanding certain struggles, or anger over symptoms having been overlooked for so long" (Fairbank, 2023).

After my twins' diagnosis, I joined a support group for parents of kids with ADHD. In this group, a few of the members have ADHD themselves. I spoke to another mom, Emily, who didn't know that she has ADHD until her little boy was diagnosed at six years old. At that point, she was already in her early thirties and had gone through some really challenging moments in her life. Unbeknownst to her, many of her most traumatic experiences were related to ADHD.

Emily gave me permission to share some of her stories. Because of undiagnosed ADHD, she dropped out of college at nineteen, had tumultuous relationships, abused alcohol, suffered from depression and anxiety, and ruined her credit score because of impulsive buying in her early to mid-twenties. After receiving her diagnosis, she felt relief and regret at the same time.

"It's comforting to finally have an explanation after spending most of my life thinking that there's just something inherently wrong with me," she told me. "At the same time, I can't help but feel sorry for my younger self. Had she known what I know now, she wouldn't have had to suffer so much."

I wanted to talk about this misconception in depth because some of you may have daughters who aren't showing signs of ADHD. Because there is evidence that ADHD may be genetic, if you have sons that have been diagnosed with ADHD, I implore you to observe your daughters as well. Additionally, even if your daughters have already been diagnosed with ADHD, you may think that they are doing just fine because there aren't many visible symptoms to indicate that they're struggling with this disorder. Remember that girls are more inattentive than hyperactive/impulsive, so their symptoms may be more internalized. It may be more difficult to detect ADHD in your daughters, but I will help you identify some key markers of the inattentive type in the next subchapter.

3. ADHD Is a Childhood Disorder

As I mentioned earlier, more recent studies have shown that ADHD symptoms can persist into adulthood, especially when an individual is not provided with effective management tools in childhood. Symptoms may manifest differently as they grow up, but the root of the problem remains the same (Caye, 2016; Di Lorenzi, 2021; Gillespie, 2023; Sibley et al., 2017).

For instance, while adults with ADHD may not throw temper tantrums like children do, that doesn't mean they no longer experience emotion dysregulation. In fact, there is evidence that adults with ADHD suffer from temperament issues such as irritability and excessive emotional responses, both of which could affect their relationships with their families, partners, colleagues, and friends (Pinzone et al., 2019).

ADHD affects adults in many other ways, such as impairments on their executive function, which negatively impacts the overall quality of their life (Thorell et al., 2019). To help them avoid such problems, we must teach our children tools and techniques that allow them to effectively manage their symptoms and, in turn, minimize the impact of ADHD in their lives. If we teach them young, it will be easier for them to carry these healthy habits as they grow up.

4. ADHD Is the Result of Poor Parenting

In my support group, we discuss the hardships we encounter as parents of kids with ADHD. By openly talking about our struggles, we can offer advice and comfort to each other. One of the things that is often brought up during our meetings is the stigma that parents of kids with ADHD face when other people witness how this disorder affects our children.

ADHD is not just a behavioral disorder. It's also not as simple as a chemical imbalance in the brain. Like I said earlier, it is a neurodevelopmental disorder, and there is actual scientific evidence that certain regions of the ADHD brain develop differently than a neurotypical brain. Particularly, studies have shown that the ADHD brain has a smaller amygdala and weaker function in the prefrontal cortex, both of which are necessary in the regulation of emotions (Horan, 2021). I already briefly mentioned that emotion dysregulation is an issue faced by children with ADHD, and this can be explained by the "architectural" structure of their brain.

Imagine willing a house to change its architecture just by your sheer desire to have a bigger bedroom or a more functional kitchen. It's impossible, right? Something doesn't just happen because we want it to. You can't expect your children to handle their emotions as well as their neurotypical peers because their brains are built differently—something that they did not choose and cannot control. However, there are ways to make your existing bedroom and kitchen better fit your needs, like getting new furniture or changing the layout, which is exactly what symptom management tools and ADHD medication can do for your children.

Aside from their brain's architecture, children, in general, have less awareness about social norms, so they are less likely to conform to "acceptable" emotional and behavioral responses when they are experiencing frustration, anger, and other similar negative emotions.

I and the other parents in my support group have admitted that, despite knowing emotion dysregulation is an unavoidable aspect of our children's disorder, it is still challenging for us to coregulate such big emotions, especially when the triggering event seems small to our adult, non-ADHD eyes. We try our best to help our children during these episodes by extending empathy and patience instead of intimidation and aggression. After all, our goal is to switch off their "fight or flight" response, which we can only do if we create a safe space for our children to express their feelings.

However, to the ignorant person, an ADHD kid experiencing emotion dysregulation may look like a spoiled child throwing a temper tantrum.

The ADHD kid lacks discipline, and if only their parents are stricter, they wouldn't be behaving in such a manner.

Strangers also roll their eyes when ADHD kids are "rowdy" because of their hyperactive symptoms. When they run around or talk too much, they get punished by some teachers at school. Social norms are created by and for neurotypicals, so those with ADHD are told to suppress their true selves in order to fit in. When people say that an ADHD child needs to behave, what they actually mean is they want that child to behave in a neurotypical manner.

"Poor parenting" does not cause ADHD. You are not spoiling or coddling your child because you choose to treat them with empathy and not intimidation, with patience and not aggression. You are not a bad parent for celebrating your child and the things that make them different from others. They, too, deserve to feel that they are normal. Just because they are different, that doesn't mean that they are wrong.

With this said, you should also be aware that "poor parenting" can aggravate existing symptoms. For instance, if parents treat their children as neurotypicals and punish them for behaving otherwise, then symptoms can worsen in the future. This kind of parenting can also lead the child to have co-occurring mental health issues like anxiety and depression. In fact, there is evidence that negligence and an authoritarian style of parenting lead to worse behavioral issues in children with ADHD (Setyanisa et al., 2022; Teixeira et al., 2015). The parents play an important role in ensuring that their child grows up with the right kind of coping mechanisms and symptom management techniques so that they can thrive as neurodivergents in our neurotypical society.

5. ADHD Medication Increases Risk for Substance Abuse

I didn't want to give my twins ADHD medication when they were first diagnosed. There were several reasons behind my hesitation. First of all, I was worried that my children would change and lose their "sparkle" because of the medication. I adored my twins and their creative, spunky, bright personalities, and I didn't want them to lose what, to me, made them special.

I was also worried that they would become dependent on the medication. What if they could no longer function without it? What if their dependence turned into addiction? I had so many unanswered questions at the time, so what did I do? I asked someone who knew more than I did—my children's psychologist.

After we discussed what ADHD medication does and how it helps children with this disorder, I quickly realized that my anxieties were based solely on ignorance and misinformation. I had read some stories online about how parents regretted giving their children Adderall because it turned them into "zombies," and these anonymous accounts influenced my opinion. Apparently, what these parents perceived as "zombie-like" behavior was just their children's hyperactive symptoms calming down because of the medication. I learned this after my children had already started taking Concerta and became visibly less hyperactive, allowing them to focus more on tasks and activities.

Additionally, my children's psychologist reassured me that ADHD medication, if taken as prescribed by a doctor, will not make them more prone to addiction in their adolescence and adulthood. In Chapter 2, we will have a more in-depth discussion about ADHD medications so you can also be reassured that this is a safe option for your children.

ADHD is a complex disorder, and for a lot of parents, navigating their child's diagnosis can feel like exploring an unknown land without a map to guide their journey. The road ahead may seem treacherous just because it is unfamiliar, and you might find yourself facing obstacles you haven't encountered before. Hopefully, this section has cleared up some doubts or questions that you have about ADHD, so you may venture into this journey with more confidence and positivity.

With that said, let's further explore what ADHD is as a neurodevelopmental disorder in the next subchapter. Particularly, we'll look into its three different subtypes and their respective symptoms.

What Are the Types of ADHD?

I briefly mentioned that ADHD has three types: the predominantly inattentive type, the predominantly hyperactive/impulsive type, and the combined type. Depending on the symptoms your child shows, they can fall under one of these three categories. It helps to know what type of ADHD your child has because you're able to formulate a more specific management strategy for them. With that said, let's answer this question: What are key markers of each type of ADHD?

Predominantly Inattentive Type

Inattention seems pretty straightforward, doesn't it? A child who is the predominantly inattentive type finds it difficult to stay focused on tasks or activities because of their short attention span. They may daydream or "space out" when the task at hand is boring, or they may become distracted when something more interesting captures their attention (CDC, 2022a; Johns Hopkins Medicine, n.d.; Seymour, 2022).

However, these are not the only manifestations of inattention in children with ADHD. Other key markers of this presentation include but are not limited to struggling to follow instructions, being forgetful, frequently making simple mistakes, and losing or misplacing things often. They also find it difficult to stay organized, plan ahead, or pay attention to details (CDC, 2022a; Johns Hopkins Medicine, n.d.a; Seymour, 2022).

Predominantly Hyperactive and Impulsive Type

As I mentioned earlier, the most recognizable symptom of ADHD is hyperactivity. Children who are always running around, talking excessively, and seem to be bursting with energy are easily identified as having this disorder. Aside from restlessness, hyperactivity also manifests as fidgeting excessively, squirming while seated or being unable to stay seated or quiet for extended periods of time, interrupting others in conversation or speaking at inappropriate times, grabbing things from other people, and being unable to stay on task or shifting from one task to another without successfully finishing any task at all (CDC, 2022a; Johns Hopkins Medicine, n.d.a; Seymour, 2022).

Despite the name of this disorder, inattentiveness and hyperactivity are not the only symptoms it presents. The third major symptom of ADHD, impulsivity, is usually overlooked by parents and caregivers simply out of ignorance. In children with ADHD, impulsivity manifests as acting without much thought. They are risk takers and have little sense of danger, if any (NHS, 2021c; Seymour, 2022).

For example, I call one of my twins a little stuntman. From a very young age, he has been doing things that always make my heart drop to the floor. When he was three years old, he would get out of his high chair and climb on top of the table if I took my eyes off of him for a split second. I switched his high chair with another that has an adjustable harness, but that didn't last for long because he started throwing tantrums at mealtime and refused to eat his food until I unfastened his harness.

At five years old, he learned to climb the pedestal sink in the bathroom and then he would flip over like Spiderman, his legs on either side of his arms and his precious head hanging just inches from the hard tiled floor. When I saw him doing this for the first time, I shrieked and nearly had a heart attack. It wasn't the last time my dear boy did this stunt to scare his poor mother, but we have since learned to redirect his daredevilish energy toward activities that are much safer (and less scary for me).

Combined Type

Lastly, the combined type pertains to those who are equally inattentive and hyperactive-impulsive. There is evidence that the combined type is the most prevalent form of ADHD, especially in adults (ADDA Editorial Team, 2023a; Johns Hopkins Medicine, n.d.).

The presentation of ADHD symptoms can change over time as your child grows up. Environmental factors can bring out certain symptoms that weren't present before. At the same time, certain symptoms may be less obvious or severe as children learn new coping techniques. Therefore, it's important to keep an eye on how their symptoms are presenting, so you can continue to calibrate their management strategy based on their specific needs.

Speaking of management strategies, what can you do to help your child navigate their diagnosis? What treatment options are available for children with ADHD? These are just some of the questions that we will answer in the next chapter.

Chapter 1 Review

- Attention-deficit hyperactivity disorder (ADHD) is a neurodevelopmental disorder that affects five to eight percent of children.

- ADHD is characterized by three main symptoms: inattention, hyperactivity, and impulsivity. The three types of ADHD are the predominantly inattentive type, the predominantly hyperactive and impulsive type, and the combined type.

- ADHD is considered a disability under the Americans With Disabilities Act of 1990. Individuals with ADHD are protected against discrimination by law.

Chapter 1 Exercise

To test your understanding of this chapter, you may answer the following questions:

1. What is neurodiversity? How can this concept help you better parent your child with ADHD?

2. What misconceptions about ADHD did you believe before your child was diagnosed with the disorder? How can you continue to challenge these misconceptions?

3. What steps have you taken to foster a positive and supportive home for your child with ADHD?

Chapter 2:

Navigating Diagnosis and Treatment

Thinking differently has given me the tools to face chaos and failure.
–Kaiya Stone

When my twins were first diagnosed with ADHD, I was more worried than I was relieved to finally have an explanation for their "bad" behaviors. I had a million questions running through my mind: Would my twins have a hard time at school? What if they couldn't keep up with their peers? Would I need to enroll them in special education? How would ADHD affect them as they grew up? Would it prevent them from succeeding in whatever they wanted to do in life?

Additionally, I was worried about my role as their parent. At the time, I had no idea how to support them. How could I help them have full, healthy, and satisfying lives despite their disorder? What if I couldn't give them the right kind of support? What if I failed to correct their "bad" behaviors? Would correcting these behaviors mean that I was suppressing who they actually were? How could I allow them to be their true selves but also make sure that they succeeded in a world that wasn't designed to cater to them and their needs?

Before we go any further, I have to mention that I never thought my twins were "bad kids" because they were showing behavioral issues. I think it's important to make that distinction because children with neurodevelopmental conditions are often stereotyped as "problem kids" who behave erratically and are difficult to raise. Many people only see their temper tantrums without knowing or understanding the underlying condition that causes these outbursts. This is an issue that we're going to explore in the next chapter when we talk about what it's actually like to parent kids with ADHD.

For now, let me share with you the advice that Mrs. Hawthorne, my children's kindergarten teacher, gave me when I told her about my anxieties regarding their diagnosis and my role as their only parent. She said:

"Alexis, you don't need to know everything now. The road ahead of you may seem intimidating from where you stand, but you still have plenty of time to learn how to best navigate it. Just do the very best you can every single day. As their mother, that's all you can really do, and that's enough."

For many of you, your children might have been recently diagnosed, and you fear the journey that your children will take from here on out. For others, you might have been on this journey with your children for quite a while now, yet you still feel lost at times. I experienced the same feelings of anxiousness, and I still go through them some days. I'm afraid worrying is simply a part of our job description as parents, regardless of whether our children are neurodivergent or neurotypical. The journey may get easier as they grow up, but the anxiety never fully disappears.

If you're also feeling overwhelmed and scared, that's okay. Your feelings are normal and valid. Whenever you feel like you're drowning in a wave of anxiety, I hope you remember Mrs. Hawthorne's advice to me. Navigate your child's diagnosis day by day, and tend to their needs the best way you can.

Yes, the road in front of you will not always be clear, but put your worries aside. I'm here as your temporary guide while you read this book, so you may get a better view of what's ahead of you. In this chapter, I will help you better understand your child's disorder by first talking about the diagnostic process, and then by going through the different treatment options and management techniques for ADHD. Through our discussion, my hope is to alleviate some of the worry and anxiety you're feeling, allowing you to focus more on taking care of your kids.

Diagnosis of ADHD

The process of diagnosing a child with any type of neurodevelopmental disorder starts at home. As parents and caregivers, we will be the first ones to see signs and symptoms of ADHD. We may also receive assistance from other adults who spend significant time with our kids, like teachers, just as Mrs. Hawthorne guided me. In any case, it is our responsibility to recognize the problem and to seek help by taking our children to a professional for a formal evaluation.

With that said, let's go through the process of diagnosing ADHD. What are the first signs and symptoms that parents should be aware of? Additionally, what criteria do professionals use to formally diagnose a child with ADHD?

The First Signs of ADHD

If you're reading this book, it's likely that your child has already been diagnosed with ADHD. In other words, you or someone close to your child may have already noticed the first signs of ADHD, which then prompted you to take your child to a specialist. I decided to write a section about the first signs of ADHD because some readers may have noticed that their child is different from their peers but are still hesitating to take them for an evaluation. It's also possible that you have other children who have not been diagnosed with the disorder, and you're curious whether ADHD runs in the family.

No matter what your situation is, it's important that you have a clear idea of the indicators of ADHD. In the previous chapter, I outlined some of the common manifestations of inattentiveness, hyperactivity, and impulsivity. These are the first signs that you would observe in a child with ADHD. If you have been noticing some of these presentations in your children for at least six months, then you should consider taking them to a professional for a formal assessment.

It also helps to educate yourself about the key developmental markers of neurotypical children so you'll more easily recognize atypical behaviors in a neurodivergent child. There are several cognitive, social and emotional, language and communicative, and movement and physical milestones that can be observed in certain age groups of children. It's important to remember that even though ADHD is a neurodevelopmental disorder, it will not only affect the child's cognitive skills. You may also find other remarkable differences in these other areas.

For example, according to the CDC (2023a), one of the key emotional milestones of a child at three years old is the ability to calm down within 10 minutes after a parent leaves them at daycare. Children with ADHD who struggle with emotion dysregulation may not be able to self-soothe within this timeframe. Based on experience, they may also have more "explosive" showcases of emotions (e.g., rolling on the floor, screaming, and throwing things while crying) because they simply do not know how to regulate the big feelings they are experiencing. To our eyes, their reaction may not be appropriate for the triggering event, but the child with ADHD doesn't realize that they are experiencing emotional dysregulation.

Another example of atypical behavior that children with ADHD may exhibit is the inability to adapt to their surroundings. More specifically, neurotypical children will be able to change their behavior to suit their environment at four years of age (CDC, 2023b). They know that they need to sit still and be quiet inside a church or a library, while they can run and scream at the playground. On the other hand, a child with ADHD may not be able to control their hyperactive symptoms even in places where they are expected to be still and quiet. They may want to keep standing even in the middle of mass or talk loudly in the library. These are common signs of hyperactivity in children with ADHD.

At five years old, a child must be able to focus "for 5 to 10 minutes during activities. For example, during story time or making arts and crafts (screen time does not count)" (CDC, 2023c). On the contrary, a child with ADHD may not be able to do so because of inattention. A neurotypical child also "follows rules or takes turns when playing games with other children" (CDC, 2023c), both of which are difficult for a child with ADHD because of inattention and impulsivity.

These are just some examples of how a child with ADHD differs from their neurotypical peers. As you can see, it is easier to recognize the first signs of the disorder if you know the developmental benchmarks of neurotypical children.

Remember, however, that a child with ADHD isn't "less than" other children their age just because they're not hitting these milestones at around the same time. Consider this: A bee in a flower field full of butterflies may appear like a nuisance to people walking by. They may even be afraid of the bee, worried that it may sting them, but they don't know that a bee only stings out of self-defense. Because people are uninformed, they may think the bee doesn't belong in the field of butterflies or that it is a danger to them. They dislike the bee because of this and avoid it as they walk through the flower field.

However, bees also pollinate the field, helping beautiful flowers to bloom, the same flowers that passersby enjoy looking at during their stroll. In the same way, a child with ADHD may be different from their peers, and they may stand out because of their differences. However, the way they are and the way they exist aren't necessarily wrong. Keep in mind what we talked about when we discussed neurodiversity in the previous chapter. Differences in development, skills, and behaviors don't make one child better than the other. The bee is just as valid as the butterflies in that flower field. It is just as beautiful, important, and precious.

The DSM-5 Diagnostic Criteria for ADHD

Clinicians and researchers use the *Diagnostic and Statistical Manual of Mental Disorders, Fifth Edition (DSM-5)* to "define and classify mental disorders, which can improve diagnoses, treatment, and research" (American Psychiatric Association, 2023). The CDC (2022c) has summarized the *DSM-5* criteria for diagnosing patients with ADHD as follows:

- For children up to 16 years old, the individual must have at least six symptoms of inattention and/or hyperactivity-impulsivity that have been present for at least six months at the time of diagnosis.

- For adolescents and adults aged 17 years old and above, the individual must have at least five symptoms of inattention and/or hyperactivity-impulsivity that have been present for at least six months at the time of diagnosis.

- Symptoms are inappropriate for the individual's level of development.

- Symptoms must have been present before the child is 12 years old and are observable in two or more settings (e.g., at home, in school, on the playground, when visiting relatives, when playing with friends, et cetera).

- Symptoms are clearly disruptive to the child's daily life (e.g., academic life, social life, et cetera).

- There are no other mental disorders that would cause or explain the child's symptoms. Symptoms are present beyond a schizophrenic or psychotic episode.

To reach a diagnosis, the child may have to go through a medical exam "to help rule out other possible causes of symptoms," and the specialist will also look at the child's "current medical issues, personal and family medical history, and school records" (Mayo Clinic Staff, 2019). Parents, guardians, and teachers may also be interviewed or asked to answer a questionnaire to provide further information about the child's behavior and symptoms. After these steps, the child may be diagnosed with one of three types of ADHD depending on the symptoms they are showing. However, the disorder's presentation may still change over time as they grow up, just like we discussed in the previous chapter (CDC, 2022c; Mayo Clinic Staff, 2019).

The Parents' Role in the Diagnostic Process

The process for diagnosing children with ADHD can be complicated because it relies heavily on the accounts of other people, like parents and teachers, whereas adults with ADHD have some level of self-awareness and can therefore self-report on the symptoms they are struggling with. Other neurodevelopmental problems can also have similar symptoms to ADHD, such as Autism Spectrum Disorder (ASD) and certain learning disabilities. For some children, their symptoms may go unnoticed until much later in life when the disruption caused by ADHD has become more severe, resulting in poor grades at school, dropping out of school, or the inability to keep a steady job.

With all of this said, parents like us have a huge responsibility to keep an observant eye on our children, the symptoms they are showing, and the disruption these symptoms cause in their lives. Children, especially very young ones like preschoolers, may not have the ability to accurately describe their symptoms to a specialist. They may not even be aware that their symptoms are causing an issue that needs to be addressed. Therefore, it is our job to speak on their behalf when they can't and to inform the specialist of the issues we have noticed.

For parents whose children haven't been formally diagnosed, here are some tips to help you during the process:

- Familiarize yourself with the developmental markers of children at different ages, as well as the different presentations of ADHD symptoms. You may also want to read about other neurodevelopmental disorders, so you're aware if the signs and symptoms you're noticing are overlapping with theirs. This allows you to easily recognize issues in your child's behavior.

- Record any possible symptoms that you have noticed in your child. Keep track of how often these behaviors are present, when and where they are present (e.g., time of day, environment, or type of activity), and how long they typically last. You should also take note of when these symptoms started, if they are disruptive to your child's life, and how they are causing disruption.

- Maintain a routine at home while you're observing your child. A routine allows you to more easily recognize unusual patterns in your child's behavior.

- Observe if there are triggers that lead to your child's behavior. For example, do they throw big tantrums when they want to skip naptime to play? Does your child get upset when you take away their devices after a previously agreed-upon time? How intensely do they react, and is there a way to pacify them?

- Initiate activities that test your child's ability to focus. For example, you can do jigsaw puzzles, read books, or bake cookies together. Take note of how long your child is able to hold their attention toward the task at hand.

- You may further test your child's attention span by first doing things they already like and then trying activities they may not be as interested in. How different are their behaviors during each task? Is their attention span considerably longer when doing tasks they are already interested in? How quickly are they distracted when you attempt to make them do things they may not like?

- If your child is attending school, contact their teachers to inquire about their behavior. Set up a meeting and request a report on their behavior if possible. You can present this report to the specialist to help them better understand your child's condition.

- If there are support groups in your area, join one. There is much to learn from other parents who are going through the same thing as you are, especially those who have been on this journey longer than you have.

The diagnostic process is important in finding the right treatment and management strategy for your child. While it can be daunting and exhausting, it is a necessary step to go through, so I hope you make use of the tips I have listed above.

Speaking of treatment and management, what options are available for your child? Let's talk about them in the next subchapter.

Treatment and Management of ADHD

ADHD, like other neurodevelopmental disorders, is not a curable condition. However, there are treatment and management options that help alleviate symptoms and significantly reduce the disruption caused by the disorder in your child's life. In this subchapter, we'll take a closer look at cognitive-behavioral therapy, pharmacotherapy, parent training, and other treatment and management methods that are designed for ADHD.

Cognitive-Behavior Therapy (CBT)

The American Psychological Association (APA, n.d.a) defines cognitive-behavior therapy as:

> a form of psychotherapy that integrates theories of cognition and learning with treatment techniques derived from cognitive therapy and behavior therapy. CBT assumes that cognitive, emotional, and behavioral variables are functionally interrelated. Treatment is aimed at identifying and modifying the client's maladaptive thought processes and problematic behaviors through cognitive restructuring and behavioral techniques to achieve change.

But how does CBT specifically help individuals with ADHD? Well, it is common for those with ADHD to fall into all-or-nothing thinking ("This has to be perfect or it is not good at all!"), emotional reasoning ("I should leave the party immediately because the host doesn't seem to like me."), and overgeneralized fortune telling ("No matter how hard

I study, I will fail this math test like all the others in the past."), among other disruptive cognitive patterns. CBT aims to challenge these thought processes that prevent them from completing tasks, maintaining good relationships, and succeeding in life. A therapist will help the patient get to the root of these disruptive cognitive patterns so they can find the most apt solution. For example, if your child shows signs of emotional reasoning, a therapist may teach them how to be less reactive so that they're not always led by their feelings or making decisions based on temporary emotions.

When my twins were younger, my boy threw fewer but more explosive tantrums than my girl. Whenever he did have episodes, there was no pacifying him. I tried everything I could to control his tantrums and co-regulate his emotions—holding him in my arms, rocking him back and forth, cooing at him, playing gentle and soothing music, guiding him to take deep breaths, offering him a snack—but nothing worked. He'd lie on the floor and scream while kicking his legs. Sometimes, he'd throw his toys across the room, and all I could do was to wait for him to get all of his feelings out of his system.

When they started going to therapy, one of the first things he learned was to hold his feelings in his hand like he's holding a ball. He'd imagine the ball of emotions getting bigger and heavier the longer he felt upset, and his goal would be to keep the ball small enough to fit in his hand. The only way to make the ball that small was to take deep and even breaths. Whenever he felt upset, he'd do this exercise. He'd pause, stretch his hands out in front of him with his palms facing the ceiling, and attempt to make the ball as small as he possibly could.

The imaginative aspect of this exercise allows him to visualize the feelings he couldn't explain or control. It also allows his brain to focus on one thing—the invisible ball of emotions on his hands—instead of falling into a disruptive thought pattern that could make his episode worse. Once the ball had gotten small enough to hold in his hands, he would have taken enough deep breaths to calm him down, and he'd be able to communicate to me why he felt upset in the first place.

Aside from challenging problematic cognitive patterns, there is scientific evidence that CBT is an effective management tool for children with various mental disorders like anxiety, depression, and ADHD. In fact, research has been done on the topic for years, including a 2010 study by Minde et al. that showed the effectiveness of CBT in reducing anxiety symptoms from moderate and severe to mild or transient in children aged three to seven years. More specifically, CBT has been shown to have a positive impact "on emotional symptoms (irritability, depression), aggressiveness, and overall functioning in children with ADHD and [emotion dysregulation]" (Vacher et al., 2020). There is also evidence that CBT can reduce anxiety symptoms in children and adolescents with ADHD (Friesen & Markowsky, 2021; León-Barriera et al., 2022).

My twins started going to therapy shortly after they were diagnosed, and they have been seeing the same child psychologist from the beginning. As they grow up and learn to self-manage their symptoms, their bimonthly sessions have gradually turned into monthly and now quarterly sessions. I also have regular meetings with their therapist, so I can get a better understanding of their current state and how I can best help them at home.

I have personally witnessed the positive impact CBT has had on my children's lives. They have learned many self-management techniques through their wonderful therapist. For instance, they are now able to recognize and communicate whenever they're upset, frustrated, or exhausted. They often use phrases like "I need a minute, Mom" or "May I have some space, please?" to let me know that they want to process their feelings by themselves before we talk about them. This simple technique has prevented many tantrums and misunderstandings.

Through CBT, they have also learned techniques to improve their attention so they can focus on schoolwork, communicate effectively with their peers so they can make and keep friends, and process their emotions in a healthy and productive manner. While my twins still sometimes struggle with their symptoms, they are better equipped to avoid and manage the disruptions that ADHD causes in their lives. I know that with time, they will also learn to cope with the symptoms they are most struggling with right now. At the same time, as their parent, I am learning new techniques to best support them as they grow and go through changes.

I can't recommend CBT enough because I personally see the positive impact it has on my twins and their daily lives. And because CBT is specific to each patient, we are able to find customized solutions to the problems they are facing at any particular time.

While CBT has many benefits and is effective in correcting problematic thought and behavioral patterns in children with ADHD, you can maximize its effects if you pair it with other treatment and management strategies such as pharmacotherapy and parent training. With the proper guidance of a specialist, I encourage you to explore these options, too.

Pharmacotherapy

The American Psychological Association (APA, n.d.b) defines pharmacotherapy as "the treatment of a disorder by the administration of drugs, as opposed to such means as surgery, psychotherapy, or complementary and alternative methods." In simpler terms, it is the use of drugs to treat disorders or, in the case of ADHD, help manage symptoms of the disorder.

There are two main types of ADHD medication: stimulant and non-stimulant drugs. In general, ADHD stimulant medications are considered "controlled," "scheduled," or "dangerous" substances in most countries because they pose a risk of misuse, dependence, or abuse if not taken as prescribed by a doctor. In the United States, stimulant medications for ADHD are categorized under Schedule II controlled substances under the *Controlled Substances Act*, which also include painkillers like OxyContin and Vicodin (Food and Drug Administration [FDA], 2023; Liao, 2017).

For many parents, the risk that comes with prescription stimulant medications for ADHD is enough for them to completely disregard the idea that their children may need them to effectively manage their symptoms. To be honest, I was hesitant at first, too. I didn't want my children to become dependent on a drug, and I thought that the risks of medicating my children far exceeded the benefits it would bring to their lives.

To ease my mind, I spoke to my twins' psychiatrist to learn more about ADHD medication. She also sent me a few links to articles so I could further educate myself about these drugs. After I did some reading, I consulted with her again to reach a decision. Ultimately, I chose to let them go on 18 milligrams of Concerta every weekday, as prescribed by their doctor, to help them focus at school.

In this section, I want us to take a deeper dive into the different types of ADHD medication. My hope is to ease your mind if you have any hesitations or fears about pharmacotherapy. At the very least, I wish to educate you about ADHD medications so you can make an informed decision with your children's doctor.

Before we proceed, I just want to reiterate that only a licensed specialist can prescribe ADHD medication. You must take your child for a consultation with a psychiatrist to get the proper prescription.

With that said, let's answer the following questions: What is the difference between stimulant and non-stimulant drugs? How do each type work? Lastly, what benefits and risks should parents and caregivers be aware of?

Stimulant ADHD Medication

Giving a hyperactive child a stimulant drug may seem counterintuitive. Wouldn't a stimulant just make them more hyperactive and unable to focus? How could it possibly help a child with ADHD manage their symptoms? When I first heard about ADHD stimulant drugs, I imagined a kid with eyes opened wide, running around and panting after taking their medication. I have also heard horror stories about people who use Adderall recreationally and without prescription because it gives them a "high" and makes them feel energized. Even though my children would be taking stimulant ADHD medication with a prescription, I was still worried about this outcome.

However, there is a reason why Adderall and other stimulant drugs are prescribed for ADHD. This type of medication actually increases the dopamine levels in the brain, which addresses the issue of deficiency that we discussed in the first chapter. Stimulant ADHD medication works "by blocking dopamine reuptake, allowing more of the chemical to stay in neurons" (Villines, 2023). Amphetamine and methylphenidate, the active ingredients of stimulant ADHD medication, also improve "central [dopamine] and [norepinephrine] activity in brain regions that include the cortex and striatum" (Faraone, 2018). As a result, an individual is able to improve focus while the drug is active in their system, allowing them to complete their tasks successfully and achieve better results in their studies (Cleveland Clinic, 2022; Faraone, 2018; Oladipo, 2021; Villines, 2021; Villines, 2023).

Multiple studies have also shown that stimulant ADHD medication can aid in "reducing the risk of suicide, lowering the rate of substance-related events, promoting better performance in school, reducing the likelihood of motor vehicle accidents and lowering criminality rates" in the long run (Villines, 2021).

There are several FDA-approved stimulant ADHD medications that your child's doctor can prescribe depending on their needs. These generic and brand names are available in the United States. However, other countries may have restrictions on which stimulant ADHD medication can be prescribed and sold, so I encourage you to search for what is legally available in your location. Of course, your best bet is to consult with a psychiatrist to know what medication is best for your child. With that said, Cleveland Clinic (2022) has listed all of the FDA-approved stimulant ADHD medication in the United States:

- Amphetamine ADHD medication
  - Amphetamine Immediate-Release
    - Amphetamine sulfate (Evekeo, Evekeo ODT)
    - Dextroamphetamine mixed salts and amphetamine (Adderall)
    - Dextroamphetamine sulfate (Zenzedi)
    - Methamphetamine hydrochloride (Desoxyn)
  - Amphetamine Extended-Release

- Amphetamine (Adzenys ER, Adzenys XR-ODT, Dyanavel XR)

- Dextroamphetamine mixed salts and amphetamine (Adderall XR)

- Dextroamphetamine sulfate (Dexedrine, ProCentra)

- Lisdexamfetamine dimesylate (Vyvanse, Vyvanse chewable)

- Mixed salts of a single-entity amphetamine (Mydayis)

- Methylphenidate Generic Names and Brands
  - Methylphenidate Immediate-Release
    - Dexmethylphenidate hydrochloride (Focalin)
    - Methylphenidate hydrochloride (Methylin chewable, Methylin Oral Solution, Ritalin)
  - Methylphenidate Extended-Release
    - Dexmethylphenidate hydrochloride (Focalin XR)
    - Methylphenidate (Cotempla XR-ODT, Daytrana patch)
    - Methylphenidate hydrochloride (Adhansia XR, Aptensio XR, Concerta, Jornay PM, Metadate CD, Metadate ER, Methylin ER, Quillichew ER, Quillivant XR, Ritalin-SR, Ritalin LA)
    - Serdexmethylphenidate and Dexmethylphenidate (Azstarys)

You might have noticed from this list that there are two categories of stimulant medication under each active ingredient, i.e. immediate-release and extended release. On average, the former is active for up to four hours, while the latter can last between six to eight hours. The specific range of active effect in the system varies depending on the drug. For example, amphetamine-based Mydayis and methylphenidate-based Adhansia XR can last up to 16 hours (Cleveland Clinic, 2022). However, Mydayis is only prescribed for patients 13 years old and above. Note also that Adhansia XR has been discontinued by its manufacturer, Adlon Therapeutics, as of July 2022 (Davydovskaya, 2019; Pesantez, n.d.).

We've talked about the benefits of these drugs to patients with ADHD, but what about the risks? Well, stimulant ADHD medication can cause tics, a decrease in appetite resulting in weight loss, growth delay in adolescents, increase in heart rate, and feelings of anxiety. As your child adjusts to the medication, they may also experience nausea and difficulties in falling and staying asleep. Moreover, some immediate-release medications may cause what is called a "rebound effect" where your child feels a sudden drop in their energy level resembling fatigue as the medication loses its effect (Cleveland Clinic, 2022; Villines, 2021).

While most of the side effects that I mentioned above disappear after a few weeks (i.e. once the body adjusts to the medication), it's still important for parents like us to be aware of the potential risks so we can be prepared. Speaking of being prepared, at the end of this section, I included some tips for parents who are considering pharmacotherapy to treat and manage their child's ADHD symptoms. This section includes advice on how to maximize the benefits and reduce the risks of stimulant ADHD medication. Before we get there, however, let's first look at the different types of non-stimulant ADHD medication.

Non-Stimulant ADHD Medication

Cleveland Clinic (2022) has also listed all the FDA-approved non-stimulant medications in the United States:

- Selective Norepinephrine Reuptake Inhibitors (SNRIs)
  - Atomoxetine hydrochloride (Strattera)

- Viloxazine (Qelbree)
- Alpha-2 Adrenergic Agonists
  - Clonidine hydrochloride (Kapvay)
  - Guanfacine hydrochloride (Intuniv)

If you remember, we talked about the neurochemical background of ADHD in Chapter 1, and norepinephrine is one of the chemicals that the ADHD brain lacks. Selective norepinephrine reuptake inhibitors work by increasing the brain's norepinephrine levels, although they are not as effective in treating ADHD symptoms as stimulant medications that increase the brain's dopamine levels. In fact, SNRIs are considered a second option in treating ADHD symptoms and given only when a patient can't take stimulants or hasn't seen improvements from stimulants (Khan, 2021; Miller, 2023; Rodden, 2023; Sissons, 2022).

Before we talk about alpha-2 adrenergic agonist medications, I want to note that selective norepinephrine reuptake inhibitors are different from serotonin-norepinephrine reuptake inhibitors, also known as antidepressants. The former specifically targets norepinephrine reuptake, while the latter targets norepinephrine *and* serotonin reuptake (Cleveland Clinic, 2023). Although technically not an ADHD medication, antidepressant SNRIs may be beneficial to some individuals, and a psychiatrist may also prescribe it alongside ADHD medication based on the symptoms your child is presenting.

Meanwhile, alpha-2 adrenergic agonist medications were originally created and marketed as blood pressure medication for adults suffering from hypertension. They were later found to increase norepinephrine levels in the brain, so now they're used to treat ADHD and other conditions including spasticity, tics, aggression, sleep problems, and fibromyalgia (Miller, 2023; Sruthi, n.d.).

In most cases, a non-stimulant medication is prescribed only after a patient has tried a stimulant medication. Intense side effects that don't go away, high risk for substance abuse, and co-occurring conditions like anxiety are some reasons as to why a psychiatrist would prescribe

SNRIs or agonists over methylphenidate or amphetamine (Miller, 2023).

Tips for Parents Considering Pharmacotherapy

Many parents are hesitant to put their children on ADHD medication because of possible side effects. I hope this chapter has eased some doubts you may have had regarding ADHD medications.

If you're leaning toward using pharmacotherapy for your child with ADHD, here are some tips to consider before and after the treatment begins:

1. (Before) **Do your research.** Congratulations! By reading this subchapter, you've made a huge step into researching ADHD medications. I'm sure most of you have more questions in mind, so I highly recommend that you do further research about the topic. Just make sure that you look into reliable sources, like peer-reviewed medical journals or web articles reviewed by actual medical professionals. Checks and balances in research studies and reporting ensure that you're getting an unbiased perspective on the benefits and risks of pharmacotherapy.

2. (Before) **Consult with your doctor.** After doing some research, you may still have some unanswered questions about pharmacotherapy. Gather all of these questions and ask your child's psychiatrist during their next appointment. My children's doctor had answered dozens of questions from me before they started taking Concerta, and her answers gave me reassurance that pharmacotherapy was the best route for them. Of course, your consultation may prove that your child's symptoms don't warrant the use of medication, so it's always best to ask for your doctor's opinion before deciding on a course of action.

3. (Before) **Inform teachers that your child will be taking ADHD medication.** For school-aged children, they will spend

most of their time on medication while at school, so you may not personally witness if the medication is leading to the results you're hoping for. You may coordinate with your child's teachers so they can inform you of any improvements, or lack thereof, they may notice in your child's behavior and academic performance.

4. (After) **Follow the prescription.** As with any type of medication, it is imperative that you follow the prescription when administering your child's ADHD medication to avoid unwanted side effects. In the beginning, I also recommend that you keep their medication away from where they can easily access it, giving them only what they need to take when they need to take it. This ensures that your child takes strictly what is prescribed by the doctor. Some children may feel like they need another dose because they can't feel the effect of the medication, while others may form a dependence when left unsupervised. Once the child has adjusted well to the medication, then you can slowly give them more independence.

5. (After) **For stimulant medications, timing is key.** Most extended-release stimulant medications last an average of eight hours in the system. After that, the child may experience a crash that resembles fatigue. If you administer the medication too early in the day, they may crash while still at school or doing after-school activities. On the contrary, if you administer the medication too late in the day, they may find it difficult to sleep at night. Therefore, consider your child's schedule when administering the medication to make sure they're taking it at the best time. If possible, it's advisable to administer the medication at the same time every day so the body adjusts well to the medication.

6. (After) **Observe, take notes, and report back to the doctor.** Adjustments to your child's prescription may be necessary depending on the side effects they're experiencing and the

improvements they're showing. Not only that, their doctor may suggest other treatment and management options to maximize the benefits your child will reap from pharmacotherapy. Therefore, it's necessary to regularly touch bases with your child's psychiatrist.

Parent Training

As much as we try to be calm, compassionate, and reasonable when our children experience emotion dysregulation or oppositional defiant disorder (ODD), we may still sometimes lose our temper and let our emotions triumph over rationality. (Briefly, ODD is a behavioral disorder that makes children "uncooperative, defiant, and hostile toward peers, parents, teachers, and other authority figures" [Johns Hopkins Medicine, n.d.b].) When this happens, we may unintentionally cause more issues, leading to worse episodes of dysregulation, more aggression, and stronger resistance from our children.

It is only natural that they react this way if they feel wronged or rejected. After all, we already know that neurodivergent children have a difficult time controlling their emotions, and our reaction may compound the negative feelings they are already experiencing. As challenging as it may be, it is always our responsibility to handle and resolve these difficult situations, especially when our children are too young to change their own behaviors.

However, to understand this responsibility and to put it into practice 100% of the time are two completely different things. When my twins turned nine years old, my boy started having more and worse dysregulated episodes. Even the slightest inconveniences—from forgetting how to tie his shoelaces to not being able to eat what he wanted for dinner—could trigger him. (I mean, I couldn't just let him eat chicken nuggets and fries every night, right?) It was particularly difficult for me to remain in control of myself and the situation whenever he threw a tantrum in public. I shared the challenges I was facing during one of my support group meetings, and another mom recommended that I undergo parent training.

Parent training equips us with tools to help manage our children's behavior and coregulate their emotions. This is done in coordination with a therapist who will guide parents through regular meetings and progress reports. Parents learn management and coregulation techniques from the therapist and practice them at home. The great thing about parent training is that it leads to personalized solutions to problems parents face in regard to caring for their child with ADHD (CDC, 2023d; Pelham & Altszuler, 2022).

Parent training has been proven to result in "fewer and less severe problematic situations related to child noncompliance, particularly for chores, homework, mealtimes, and peer interactions. Parents also reported significantly reduced stress related to parenting a child with ADHD" (Ciesielski et al., 2020). In other words, not only is parent training helpful to your child, but it will also benefit you.

Other Management Methods

In my opinion, cognitive-behavioral therapy, pharmacotherapy, and parent training are the most effective treatment and management methods for ADHD. A strategy combining these three methods has resulted in the best outcomes for my twins, but I recognize that every child is different. Your child may need additional methods to help with their symptoms.

If this is something you're looking into, or if you just want to be prepared to implement another strategy to help manage and treat your child's symptoms, here are three other methods that you can consider: family therapy, social skills training, and physical exercise.

Family Therapy

ADHD symptoms do not only affect the individual with the disorder—it can also impact other members of the family, especially when there are intense external symptoms and co-occurring conditions like emotion dysregulation, ODD, and other behavioral issues.

It is also common for children with ADHD to have rejection sensitive dysphoria (RSD), which is a high sensitivity to perceived rejection that stems from emotion dysregulation. RSD can lead to an insecure attachment style in children with ADHD. Both RSD and an insecure attachment style can cause strained relationships between the child with ADHD and their parents, as well as their siblings (Carr et al., 2020; Ewan, 2023). We will further discuss RSD in Chapter 4, when we talk about how to nurture our children's emotional well-being.

Family therapy provides a safe and constructive space for family members to discuss how ADHD affects everyone. Through these open conversations, the family can find a way to reduce the impact of ADHD on the family unit as a whole. Family therapy also creates room for parents to build a more secure attachment with their child who has ADHD (Carr et al., 2022; Lovering, 2022).

Social Skills Training

Emotion dysregulation, RSD, and an insecure attachment style also hinders children with ADHD from connecting and forming lasting friendships with their peers. The behavioral presentations of their symptoms also adds another layer of challenge in terms of socializing. For example, talking over others, the inability to wait for their turn, and overzealousness may appear rude to those without the disorder.

To help your child build friendships and maintain relationships, you may opt to enroll them in a social skills training class where they will learn age-appropriate techniques to communicate and relate with their peers. Through social skills training, your child will also be taught self-management techniques so they can better regulate their emotions and prevent issues when interacting with others (Lovering, 2022; Storebø et al., 2019).

Physical Exercise

Physical exercise is a natural way to trigger the release of hormones, including dopamine and norepinephrine, which the ADHD brain lacks.

It also releases other happy hormones like serotonin, which improves mood like dopamine, and lowers stress hormones like cortisol and epinephrine (APA, 2020; Mehren et al., 2020).

Additionally, there is scientific evidence that acute physical exercise mitigates some ADHD symptoms like inattentiveness and executive dysfunction. It is also proven to reduce disruptive behavioral issues and moodiness, as well as improve peer functioning, working memory, and motor performance (Mehren et al., 2020).

Little League, swimming, soccer, ballet, gymnastics, taekwondo—these are just some examples of physical activities that your children may find interesting. Not only do these activities facilitate exercise, but they also give your child a chance to socialize with their peers. Moreover, there is a sense of accomplishment that comes with learning new skills, which can be good for their self-esteem.

There is no cure for ADHD—this is the reality that we must quickly accept after our children are diagnosed with this disorder. However, I hope that in this chapter, I was able to show you that treatment and management of symptoms are possible. With the right strategy, your child's condition can improve.

Chapter 2 Review

- The most common treatment and management methods for ADHD are cognitive-behavior therapy (CBT), pharmacotherapy, and parent training. A strategy incorporating a combination of these three methods will significantly improve the life of a child with ADHD.

- Cognitive-behavior therapy (CBT), also known as talk therapy, helps children identify problematic cognitive patterns that lead to behavioral issues, gives them space to process their thoughts, feelings, and experiences, and equips them with proper coping skills and management techniques.

- Pharmacotherapy involves the administering of medication to treat and manage ADHD symptoms. There are two types of ADHD medication.

    ○ Stimulant ADHD medications come in either an instant-release or extended-release. They are made with either methylphenidate or amphetamine as their active ingredient.

    ○ Non-stimulant ADHD medication comes in two forms: selective norepinephrine reuptake inhibitors (SNRIs) or alpha-2 adrenergic agonists, both of which boost norepinephrine levels in the brain.

- Other management methods for ADHD include family therapy, social skills training, and physical exercise. Each of these methods targets specific aspects (symptoms and impacts) of ADHD, so parents must consider their situation to decide whether to implement additional steps.

Chapter 2 Exercise

To help you get started on finding the right treatment and management strategy for your child with ADHD, you may answer the following questions:

1. Has your child been seeing a therapist regularly?

    a. If yes, in what ways has cognitive-behavior therapy helped with their symptoms?

    b. If not, based on your understanding of cognitive-behavior therapy from this chapter, do you think it could help your child with their symptoms? In what ways would CBT benefit them?

2. Is your child taking medication for ADHD?

    a. If yes, in what ways has pharmacotherapy helped your child with their symptoms?

    b. If not, are you considering trying pharmacotherapy for ADHD?

        i. If yes, list all of your concerns and questions about ADHD medications, and make sure to discuss them with your child's doctor during their next appointment.

        ii. If not, what hesitations do you have about ADHD medications? What risks are you wary of? Would you be willing to discuss these concerns with your child's doctor?

3. Have you gone through parent training for ADHD?

    a. If yes, in what ways has parent training helped you provide care and support for your child with ADHD?

    b. If not, based on your understanding of parent training from this chapter, do you think parent training will help you better care for and support your child with ADHD? In what ways will parent training be beneficial to you and your child?

4. Does your child need additional help in managing their ADHD symptoms? Among the three other management methods that we discussed in this chapter, which do you think will be most beneficial to your child and why?

5. Are there other management and treatment options not discussed in this chapter that you think your child may need? What are they and what results do you hope to achieve through them (e.g., special education for children with co-occurring

learning disabilities, antidepressants for children with co-occurring depressive disorder, et cetera)?

Chapter 3:

Parenting a Child with ADHD

The thing about parenting rules is there aren't any.
That's what makes it so difficult.
–Ewan McGregor

In my support group, I have met many kinds of people. Although we all have children with ADHD, we also face different challenges in our daily lives. There are some whose children require additional help because of co-occurring conditions like ASD and dyslexia. Meanwhile, there are others who struggle with correcting behavioral issues in their children. Despite their best efforts, emotion dysregulation continues to be a big problem in their households, affecting not only the child with ADHD but also their siblings. There are a few who worry about their finances because their health insurance doesn't cover the cost of ADHD medication and therapy.

ADHD adds another layer of concern for parents like us who are already balancing the many responsibilities involved in raising healthy and happy children. We're not only thinking of their basic needs because children with ADHD also require special attention and care. For parents who also have neurotypical kids, they worry about how each child feels to prevent the neurotypical child from feeling left out or thinking that their neurodivergent sibling is more important.

I don't think other people will be able to truly understand what it's like to parent a child with ADHD. I mean, even I could never fully understand what other parents in my support group are going through—I can only empathize because we have similar struggles. However, it is only through open conversations that we can seek support, share ideas, and find solutions.

We don't need to hide the "ugly" parts of parenting children with ADHD. Doing so would only add to the stigma surrounding this disorder. To me, at least, keeping our struggles a secret somehow implies that our children's disorder is a burden that we need to hide from others. But when we openly talk about the reality of parenting neurodivergent children, we normalize their disorder while making room for others to share their stories without shame.

I have included this chapter in this book exactly for this purpose. I want parents like us to have a safe space to talk about our common struggles, so we may find comfort and support from one another. Aside from looking at the challenges faced by parents of children with ADHD, I'm also sharing with you in this chapter some coping mechanisms that have personally worked wonders for me.

Common Struggles of Parents

In my support group meetings, I've noticed a few main things that parents of children with ADHD commonly struggle with: hypervigilance, chronic stress, trauma, and other mental health issues. Let's discuss each before exploring how to avoid and overcome them in the next subchapter.

Hypervigilance

Right before and after my children were diagnosed with ADHD, I was always on edge—over-analyzing every single thing they did and wondering if every behavior was a sign of the disorder. I kept a close eye on my twins (way too close, my friends would argue), and it reached a point where I couldn't focus on anything else but them. I had tunnel vision, and it was like I was always bracing myself for the worst—the worst being that ADHD ruined my children's bright futures, and I would fail as their mother to protect them from disaster.

While worrying about my children, I was unconsciously clenching my teeth all the time, and I would only catch myself doing so when my jaws started to hurt. I also found it difficult to sleep at night because a thousand thoughts, and a thousand more questions, would circle inside my head as soon as I lay in bed. I started falling behind at work, much to my embarrassment. Fortunately, I had very supportive and understanding supervisors and colleagues at my job.

The constant worrying took a toll not only on my mental health but also my physical health. For weeks, I was incredibly fatigued, and I found myself having to drag my body out of bed every morning. Simple activities like vacuuming, doing laundry, and playing with my children easily made me feel out of breath. I fell ill at some point, so my sister had to come spend her weekend nursing me back to health and taking care of the twins.

The constant state of worry that I was stuck in is called hypervigilance. It is defined as "a state of abnormally heightened alertness, particularly to threatening or potentially dangerous stimuli" (APA, n.d.c). In terms of parenting a child with ADHD, this can involve a constant state of giving yourself over for your child's needs, which in turn can lead to anxiety, physical exhaustion, and financial strain. Hypervigilance can also cause issues in your relationships with other people, like your spouse and neurotypical children, if you're focusing all of your attention on your child with ADHD.

Back when I was less informed about ADHD, I considered the disorder a danger to my twins, triggering my motherly instinct to protect them, which then resulted in hypervigilance and the health issues I experienced soon after. A domino effect left me sick and fatigued for weeks.

Like I've said previously, worrying is a normal part of our jobs as parents, but there should be a limit to our concerns if we want to avoid more serious problems like chronic stress, mental health issues, and physical illness. Hypervigilance will not help us protect our children— on the contrary, it will only prevent us from performing our duties well.

To avoid hypervigilance, the first step is to recognize when it is happening to you. At the end of this chapter, you will find some questions for self-reflection that will help you realize if you're being hypervigilant about your child's disorder. In the next subchapter, you will also find some advice on how to overcome hypervigilance.

Chronic Stress

The World Health Organization (WHO, 2023) defines stress as "a natural human response that prompts us to address challenges and threats in our lives." Meanwhile, the APA (n.d.d) defines it as "the physiological or psychological response to internal or external stressors" that "involves changes affecting nearly every system in the body, influencing how people feel and behave." In simpler terms, stress is our natural response to a threat or trigger, and it is necessary for survival. It allowed our predecessors to identify when a threat was near, assess how dangerous it was, and then decide whether to fight or take flight (Lu et al., 2021).

As parents, our role involves many stressors because we are no longer only responsible for ourselves—we also become responsible for the safety, health, and happiness of our children. It is a huge responsibility to care for another human being's life. Threats to their well-being are also a threat to us.

For instance, when our children are sick, it's natural for us to feel stressed. When they get a fever, we keep a close eye on them, constantly checking if their temperature is going up or down and making sure that they're taking their medicine on time. After a few days, when their fever is gone and they're back to good health, the stressor also goes away.

With a condition like ADHD, however, the stressor doesn't disappear because the disorder is incurable. There is no medicine that can make it go away, and our children will have to live with it for the rest of their lives. The realization that ADHD is a lifelong condition can lead to chronic stress for many parents, myself included, especially when the diagnosis is still fresh. Parents who have just joined my support group usually come into our meetings with this problem. Not being able to do something to cure the disorder often leads to feelings of helplessness, and the inability to remove the stressor is what leads to chronic stress.

However, with the proper treatment and management strategy, your child will be able to live normally with ADHD in time. With your guidance, they will learn coping strategies and techniques as they grow up. They may have to take a different path from their neurotypical peers, but they will learn to navigate this world as neurodivergent individuals.

This may seem impossible to some of you now, but so many people with ADHD have grown up as successful and happy adults. Athletes Simone Biles and Michael Phelps, director Greta Gerwig, musicians David Grohl and Reneé Rapp, actors Emma Watson and Mark Ruffalo, and TV host Trevor Noah all have ADHD (ADDitude Editors, 2023b). There are also normal people in various industries who have learned to live with ADHD, refusing to let it be a hindrance and instead using it to succeed in their chosen fields.

In the next subchapter, I will give you more practical advice on how to deal with chronic stress that stems from your child's disorder. For now, let me remind you of the advice that Mrs. Hawthorne gave me when my twins were first diagnosed. As parents, all we can really do is to try our best, and the fact that you're reading this book right now is proof that you're trying. Your willingness to learn means that you care about your child's happiness and well-being. For that, you deserve to be recognized and commended. You're doing well! Keep it up!

Trauma

When there is public discourse about ADHD, the focus is mainly on inattentiveness and hyperactivity as symptoms of this disorder, perhaps due to the name of this condition. Impulsivity is usually omitted from the conversation because people are unaware that it is also a symptom that has a great impact on affected individuals. Aside from impulsivity, there are other aspects of ADHD that people don't usually talk about, one of them being emotion dysregulation.

I have already brought up emotion dysregulation quite a few times in this book, and we haven't even properly defined it yet. (That's coming up in Chapter 4.) I always talk about it because I feel like it's one aspect of ADHD and other neurodivergent conditions that is often overlooked by people who are unfamiliar with these disorders. When a stranger sees a non-neurotypical child throwing a tantrum in the middle of a grocery aisle because their parent refused to get them a sugary cereal, it's easy for them to chalk that up to bad parenting.

"Look at that spoiled kid," they might say. They might even comment on how inadequate we are as parents that we can't control our child's behavior in public.

I recognize that most people will be unaware that our children have a condition because ADHD is an "invisible disorder," meaning it doesn't have any physical presentations. A child with ADHD will appear neurotypical to an unknowing eye, and so they label behavioral presentations of the disorder as "bad" and the child as "spoiled" or "misbehaved."

Despite recognizing this, I know that the perception of other people regarding neurodivergent conditions can cause trauma not only to the child with the disorder but also to us, their parents. Some parents of neurodivergent kids receive harsh criticisms even from their close friends and relatives. The judgment, blame, and unsolicited advice we receive from other people are enough to cause emotional scars and to damage our mental health.

I have encountered people like this, and I'm sure most of you also have. Unfortunately, there's always going to be another stranger who will tap us on the shoulder and say, "You need to discipline your child more," when they see our children "misbehaving" even when they know nothing about our lived reality.

In the beginning, I used to explain my children's condition to strangers who would stare and comment. I have long since let go of trying to change their opinions. When my children have emotionally dysregulated episodes in public, the least of my concerns is what other people might be thinking. My primary goal is always to coregulate my children's emotions, make them feel safe, and help them calm down. I focus only on them.

However, it wasn't easy reaching this point of indifference toward other people's opinions. Admittedly, I used to feel embarrassed whenever one or both of my twins would throw a tantrum at the supermarket, the mall, or a restaurant. My instinct was to step out or to take them to the restroom, away from prying eyes, until they calmed down, as if I was hiding them. I didn't realize this back then, but I was unintentionally passing the shame onto my children by doing so. I was sending the message: "Your feelings are shameful, and therefore I must hide you."

Trauma has a way of making one feel ashamed. We internalize the judgment of others and turn it into self-blame. As a result, whether intentional or not, we add to the stigma surrounding our children's disorder by prioritizing other people's opinions and forcing our children to conform to social norms that don't fit them. And like a vicious cycle, this forced conformity becomes a source of trauma for parents, too, because it makes us feel like we've failed in this role.

If this is something you've experienced, I see you. I feel you. You are not alone, and we are going to work through this together in the next subchapter.

Mental Health Issues

Hypervigilance, chronic stress, and trauma can lead to more serious mental health issues for parents of children with ADHD. Several research studies conducted through the years have examined the relationship between the parents' depression and their children's ADHD symptoms. In 2007, Musa and Shafiee found that mothers of children with ADHD have higher levels of depression, anxiety, and stress. Additionally, Mazzeschi et al. (2019) found that both fathers and mothers of children with ADHD are more likely to have depressive symptoms.

A mom in my support group—let's call her Janice—never suffered from any mental health disorders until her son—let's call him Flynn—started showing severe signs of ADHD at seven years old. Particularly, his hyperactive symptoms were causing issues not only at home but also at school. He was always running around, unable to sit still. If an adult tried to stop him, he would yell at them. It didn't matter if it was his parents or teachers—he would scream at them and sometimes use profanities that he heard from older kids in their apartment complex.

Flynn had obvious signs of ODD, which is common among children with ADHD. According to the CDC (2023e), "ODD usually starts before eight years of age, but can also occur in adolescents." As I mentioned in the previous chapter, ODD causes children to behave defiantly toward authority figures such as parents and teachers.

Janice had to pull Flynn out of school after he cursed and threw his backpack at a teacher. She told me it was one of the hardest decisions she had to make in her entire life, adding, "I didn't want my son to fall behind, but what else could I have done? I knew I had made the right decision, but it was still difficult. I felt like such a failure, like I had let him down somehow. I felt lost, too. I didn't know what to do. How could I correct his behaviors when he wouldn't listen to me? Was it even possible?"

Flynn was out of school for a whole year while he was undergoing behavioral therapy. At the same time, Janice fell into depression because she felt like she failed as his mother. She said, "I had thoughts that I've never had before, really scary thoughts, thoughts that I'm too ashamed to say out loud."

There was a time when Janice couldn't get out of bed. Their house slowly fell into disarray—dirty dishes and laundry began piling up, Flynn's toys were scattered in every room of the house, and they were eating fast food almost every day because she was too depressed to cook. At the time, her husband was deployed in the army, so she didn't have anyone to help her do these chores. The state of their house worsened her condition, making her fall deeper into depression. In her mind, she wasn't only failing as Flynn's mother, but she was also failing as a wife and a homemaker.

Eventually, Janice's husband encouraged her to see a therapist. It took her another month before booking an appointment. After seeing a doctor, she was prescribed antidepressants which, along with regular therapy sessions, really worked to make her feel better. It also helped to see Flynn slowly getting better at managing his behavior and emotions. Fortunately, Janice was able to overcome her depression.

Her story shows us the importance of taking care of our mental health. When our mental health is not in a good condition, we're not able to fulfill our parental responsibilities. As much as possible, we need to prevent the issue before it begins, so let's talk about effective coping mechanisms for parents.

Coping Mechanisms for Parents

Like I said at the beginning of this chapter, all of us are facing different challenges in our daily lives though we may have common struggles. Some children with ADHD present more severe symptoms that are disruptive not only to them but also to the entire family unit. For others, their symptoms may not even be noticeable, and so the disorder is only disruptive to the individual.

Acknowledging these differences, I've listed four coping mechanisms for parents that will work in any situation: establishing a routine, setting realistic goals, making time for oneself, and seeking help when needed. These will lay a solid foundation for you no matter what symptoms your children are presenting or how severe they may be.

Establish a Routine

Because the ADHD brain craves dopamine, it is often driven by interest and hijacked by impulse, which is why individuals with ADHD are easily distracted. Without a clear routine, they will likely do whatever they feel like at any given moment in time, which prevents them from completing tasks that they may find boring or uninteresting.

These tasks may include doing household chores (e.g., tidying up toys and washing dishes), taking care of their hygiene (e.g., showering and brushing teeth), and studying.

From the perspective of a parent, having to repeatedly remind your child to do basic tasks significantly adds to your mental load. Conflicts may also arise if your child has ODD and refuses to do as they are told. Don't underestimate the cost of mental and emotional labor to your overall health—things that may not seem like a big deal can easily build up and lead to chronic stress.

Establishing a routine as early in your child's life as possible is essential in preventing these problems. For young children, gamifying their daily routines by using colorful visual aids and a point system make boring chores more exciting. You can assign stars to every task they need to accomplish every day and reward them with something they like when they reach a certain number of stars.

Let's say brushing their teeth gains them one star, taking a bath gains them two stars, taking an afternoon nap gains them three stars, and tidying up their toys after playtime gains them five stars. If they're able to reach thirty stars at the end of the week, you'll take them out for ice cream. If they reach forty stars, you'll let them use their iPad ten more minutes every day the week after.

It's up to you to assign points to each task and to gauge which rewards will most motivate your child. You may also change the point and reward system when you notice that your child is no longer as motivated to do their tasks. As your child grows up, you may also add new tasks to their board, like more household chores and a longer study time. Changing things up once in a while adds novelty to the game, which is something the ADHD brain craves. You can make adjustments to the gamified system as necessary to motivate your child to complete their tasks and stick to their routine.

Set Realistic Goals

After receiving their child's diagnosis, some parents go into high gear to implement a treatment and management strategy that they think will work for their child. They may try too many things at once and become too strict in enforcing their strategy. "If we can just make our child follow the plan," they'll say, "then they'll be better in no time." They will look at what other parents are doing and forget that ADHD affects children differently. They may form goals that are unrealistic because they look at the success other parents have achieved with their children, using techniques that aren't applicable to their child's specific situation.

However, this mindset often leads to disappointment, as children with ADHD can be quite unpredictable. Because the ADHD brain is interest-based, there will be days when the child won't want to stick to the plan their parents have set up. They may even throw a tantrum if they feel forced to do something they don't want to do. If this happens often, the child may completely abandon the treatment and management strategy, no matter how hard the parents try to get them back on track.

Not only is this mindset harmful to the child with ADHD, but it also leads to disappointment for the parents. If the child refuses to cooperate and shows no signs of improvement, they may feel stressed and disheartened, which can lead to the issues we discussed in the previous subchapter.

Let me demonstrate what I mean by giving an example. If a parent says, "My child will adapt to this routine in three weeks," they may become strict in implementing the routine even when one or two steps may trigger the child's emotional dysregulation. And what happens if the child doesn't achieve this goal? Will they extend the trial to four weeks or change the routine completely? Will they be stricter? Will they get even stricter?

While it's true that establishing a clear routine helps your child complete daily tasks, you don't have to be too strict in enforcing the routine, especially in the beginning. Building healthy habits takes time and patience, and a child who has issues with inattentiveness, hyperactivity, impulsivity, emotional dysregulation, and ODD, among other effects of ADHD, will require more effort from their parents to guide them toward a good routine.

We must keep in mind the unpredictability of ADHD and try to make accommodations when necessary. If we give our children some allowances, they will see that we care not only about their condition but also about their feelings. This is necessary if we want them to be as cooperative as possible while we guide them toward our desired goal. Both on a day-to-day and long-term basis, we need to set realistic goals for our children and ourselves.

Make Time for Yourself

Self-care is very important for our mental health. However, many parents feel guilty when they make time for themselves, and I admit that I used to be one of those people. As a single mother, I had the mindset that I should dedicate my life first to my children and second to my work.

My sole purpose was to care and provide for my kids, so it only made sense to set aside what I thought were selfish interests. I believed I had to ignore my individuality to be a good mother and to neglect my own needs to fulfill my role. I took exhaustion as a sign of accomplishment—I wore chronic fatigue and stress around my neck like a medal. "I'm doing a great job!" was both a self-congratulatory statement and a mask that hid the burnout slowly eating me from the inside out.

In the previous subchapter, I told you how I fell ill because of hypervigilance. My body literally gave up on me because I wouldn't take a break. I remember how my sister, who took care of me while I was sick, sat me down to give me a reality check.

"You should rest, Alexis. You're not taking care of yourself," she said, but I couldn't hear what she was saying. I kept going until the burnout turned into mild depression, and only then did I realize what was actually happening. I felt disconnected from reality. I wasn't fully present at home or at work, so I wasn't able to perform my responsibilities well. As the saying goes, you can't pour from an empty cup. We can't be of service to others if there is nothing left for us.

Self-care doesn't have to be complicated or time-consuming. Personally, my self-care activity of choice is yoga, which I do for an hour every day, usually at home. I may go to a class once in a while if I can find someone to watch the twins or schedule it at the same time as their therapist appointment, but it is an exercise that I can easily do in my bedroom before preparing for bed. I also consider my morning coffee runs to be a form of self-care because it gives me time to walk in nature and soak up the sun. Now and then, I drop off the twins at their aunt's so they can play with their cousins, which gives me an opportunity to spend a whole day doing things I love.

What about you? What can you do to care for yourself on a daily basis? Taking a bubble bath, meditating, and going to the gym are some examples of self-care activities that you can try. For some, stocking a secret cabinet with snacks for when you need a little pick-me-up is a good idea. (By "some," I mean me! I have my own stash of snacks that my twins don't know about!) Since sugar can exacerbate hyperactiveness in children with ADHD, you might want to hide your favorite chocolate and candy bars. Nothing wrong with that.

Seek Help When Needed

My sister and I weren't close growing up. Even as adults, we didn't really connect on a deep level. It wasn't until we both had kids that we formed a tight bond. Motherhood somehow made us more understanding of each other, and now we rely on each other when the going gets tough.

As I mentioned, my sister sometimes takes my kids when I need a day off from parenting. Of course, I return the favor and take her kids for a day when she's the one who needs a break. We're able to take care of ourselves because we know we can seek help when we need to.

Aside from my sister, my support group has been invaluable. I'm able to find comfort from other parents who are facing similar challenges, which has given me a lot of strength when I'm struggling to manage my children's symptoms. Our meetings are a safe space for me to not only vent my frustrations but to also receive feedback and advice.

It's not embarrassing to seek help when you need it. In fact, it takes extreme courage to admit that you can't do everything by yourself. Even those who have spouses need a support system to share their burdens with so that their child's disorder doesn't put a strain on the marriage. With all of this said, I hope you can also find a community that can understand and help you during your time of need.

Parenting a child with ADHD brings unique challenges into our lives. Aside from those I listed above, you may also consider seeing a therapist to help you come up with effective coping mechanisms that will help you navigate your child's disorder with more ease.

Chapter 3 Review

- Parents of children with ADHD face another layer of challengers that lead to four common struggles: hypervigilance, chronic stress, trauma, and mental health issues like anxiety and depression.

- Parents of children with ADHD should take advantage of coping mechanisms that prevent these problems from happening in the first place. Establishing a routine, setting realistic goals, making time for oneself, and seeking help when needed can be helpful in maintaining a healthy mind.

- Taking care of your mental health is just as important as taking care of your child. When your mental health is not in good condition, you're unable to fulfill your parental responsibilities the best way you can.

Chapter 3 Exercises

To help you assess the current state of your mental health in relation to parenting a child with ADHD, you may answer the following questions (Grant, 2015; Rowden, 2022):

- Are you hyperalert to threats, real or imagined?

- Do you always feel tense or panicked?

- Is your heartbeat at an elevated rate?

- Do you feel restless most, if not all, of the time?

- Are you chronically fatigued?

- Is it difficult for you to fall asleep at night? If yes, why?

- Is it difficult for you to concentrate even on simple tasks?

- Are you irritable?

- Are you eating way less or way more than usual?

- Do you have migraines or body pains that seemingly come from nowhere?

- Are you constantly thinking about your child and their condition? Are these thoughts disruptive to your daily life and ability to perform tasks?

- Do you "hover" around your child to see if they're behaving appropriately (e.g., listening to phone conversations, reading their messages, following them around during playdates, et cetera)?

- Aside from your child's condition, can the symptoms you've identified through the above questions be explained by some other stressful event in your life? If yes, what could it be?

If you answered yes to most of these questions, you might be experiencing parental anxiety, depression, and chronic stress stemming from hypervigilance and trauma. Please employ the coping mechanisms we discussed earlier in this chapter to prevent worse outcomes and always take care of yourself.

Chapter 4:

Nurturing Emotional Well-Being

When parents offer their children empathy and help them to cope with negative feelings like anger, sadness, and fear, parents build bridges of loyalty and affection.
—John M. Gottman

A child at my local grocery store was lying in the middle of the canned goods aisle, kicking and crying. His mother crouched beside him with a worried expression, begging him to calm down. She looked visibly upset. Whenever she tried to pick him up, he would swing his arms and scream. Other shoppers passed by them like they were avoiding the hysterical child and his exhausted mom. Some looked at the pair sympathetically, while others shook their heads and rolled their eyes.

A few minutes passed, and the manager of the grocery store approached the mother. *Finally*, she thought, *someone's here to help me!*

However, the manager tapped her on the shoulder and said, "Ma'am, I'm afraid I'm going to have to ask you to leave. Your child is causing a disturbance to the other customers."

The mother was shocked and embarrassed as shoppers had come to watch her be reprimanded. As if the boy had sensed her embarrassment, he stopped crying and sat up, tugging at her mother's sleeve. She looked at him with teary eyes and said, "It's okay, baby. Come on. Let's go home."

On the car ride home, the boy kept glancing at his mother in the rearview mirror as if mustering the courage to say something. A minute passed by, and then two, and then five. A few miles from home, the boy started crying again, although it wasn't as volatile as it was earlier. The tired mother pulled to the side of the road to ask the child what was wrong. Between sobs, he said, "I'm sorry, Mommy."

If you haven't already guessed, I was the mother in this story. My son had quite a few episodes in public when he was younger, and the ending was almost always the same: We would receive judgmental stares from strangers, and he'd later apologize even though he didn't fully understand the situation. I'd explain to him that he didn't need to apologize and that I'd help him practice controlling his emotions.

Now that he's older, my son has learned how to better regulate his emotions, thanks to years of therapy, medication, and other treatment and management methods we have employed. However, this doesn't mean that he no longer experiences emotion dysregulation. Together with his therapist, we are constantly working on finding coping mechanisms that work whenever he goes through an episode.

As a parent, I can see the great impact that ADHD has on my twins' emotions, and it is one of the biggest challenges they continue to face. I'm sure many of you have also observed the same in your children, so let's talk about what we can do to nurture our children's emotional well-being.

Effects of ADHD on Emotion

At first glance, inattentiveness, hyperactivity, and impulsivity may not seem like they have an effect on your child's emotional well-being. However, neurological and social contexts both show us that ADHD does have a great impact on an individual's emotions. Let's look more closely at the effects of ADHD on emotion before we talk about the different ways we can mitigate them.

Emotion Dysregulation

For young children, the clearest sign of ADHD's impact on emotion is dysregulation. While it's normal for children to sometimes throw tantrums when they're upset, ADHD can augment negative emotions even when the triggering event seems insignificant to others. They also show age-inappropriate responses to triggers. From an external point-of-view, their reaction would seem exaggerated. For example, an eight-year-old neurotypical child will know to hold their upset feelings until the family gets home from the grocery store before expressing their frustration, whereas a child with ADHD of the same age may throw a tantrum while still shopping.

If we look at the ADHD brain from a neurophysiological perspective, we can see that the areas of the brain that are affected by the disorder are those that regulate emotion, such as the amygdala and prefrontal cortex. There is less brain activity and reduced surface area in these parts of the brain in individuals with ADHD, which leads to decreased emotional recognition, processing, and regulation (Chen, 2023; Scutti, 2017; Soler-Gutiérrez, 2023; Van Dessel et al., 2019).

Rejection Sensitive Dysphoria

Although rejection sensitive dysphoria (RSD) is not a formal medical diagnosis, it is "one of the most common and disruptive manifestations of emotional dysregulation" that individuals with ADHD experience (Dodson, 2023). RSD can cause individuals to have strong adverse responses—whether internalized, externalized, or both—to criticism, whether constructive or not, and rejection, whether it may be real or perceived (Babinski et al., 2019; Dodson, 2023; Ewan, 2023).

There are several theories as to why children with ADHD experience RSD. Aside from the neurophysiological reasons behind emotion dysregulation that we discussed earlier, "kids with ADHD hear 20,000 critical (or corrective) messages" before they turn twelve years old, which can negatively impact their self-esteem (Ewan, 2023). RSD can lead to emotional outbursts, social isolation, and negative self-perception and self-talk. In worse cases, it may even lead to thoughts of self-harm (Dodson, 2023).

Lower Self-Esteem

Self-esteem is a reflection of our own self-perception, but our self-perception is highly influenced by three factors: 1) how we perceive ourselves in comparison to others, 2) how we are perceived by others, and 3) how we think we are perceived by others. In all three measures, a condition like ADHD can impact an individual's self-esteem.

To demonstrate, consider this: Children with ADHD may struggle at school because of their symptoms, which can then prompt them to compare their performance to their neurotypical classmates who are doing much better. Negative statements like, "I'm so stupid! Why can't I do this right?" may become a common part of their internal dialogue. They may think their intellect and abilities are inferior because they don't fully comprehend how ADHD affects important cognitive functions. In simpler terms, ADHD can lead to the devaluation of oneself in comparison to others.

When it comes to external perception and self-assessment of external perception, we can look at how ADHD affects one's ability to connect with other people. After all, humans are social beings, just like most species in the animal kingdom. We crave a sense of belonging. We want to be accepted and loved by others for who we are. Therefore, when we feel rejected or ostracized, we take it as a sign that there is something wrong with us.

To some extent, children with ADHD are aware that they are different from their peers, although they may not have a good understanding of what makes them different. Judgment from others, especially adults and authority figures, can also send a message that the way they exist is not just different but also bad, and so they must change in order to be accepted by those around them.

The social stigma surrounding ADHD and neurodivergence at large can negatively impact a child's self-esteem. It forces individuals with ADHD to mask their neurodiversity and mimic how others behave even if that means that they can't be their authentic selves. The self becomes less important than acceptance, and individuals with ADHD begin to prioritize other people's opinions over their own needs and wants.

Poor Social Skills

Socialization is vital to the survival of our species. We are hard-wired to be social creatures because it allows us to find suitable partners with whom we can procreate. It also ensures that we belong in a thriving community that can provide us protection and resources. I think this is why socialization is important to our individual self-esteem. It is a primal instinct to connect with others so we can continue the existence of humankind.

However, changing social norms can cause certain individuals to isolate themselves. For instance, there is a theory that ADHD symptoms would have made an individual in the Stone Age an effective hunter and gatherer (Hammer, 2023). Hyperactivity would have someone running around in search of game for hours! Can you imagine how stocked the cave would be if the hunter had ADHD? Those with ADHD are also generally curious individuals, which is a necessary trait for exploration.

In those times, individuals with ADHD might have been praised and celebrated by their communities. On the contrary, social stigma now surrounds ADHD and its symptoms because of current societal norms, which can cause affected individuals to isolate themselves to avoid criticism and rejection. Additionally, emotion dysregulation, RSD, and low self-esteem can hinder children with ADHD from forming meaningful relationships with their peers. These issues can compound each other, leading to poor social skills. Consequently, poor social skills lead to social isolation, whether by choice or by rejection, which also negatively impacts our children's emotional well-being.

How to Nurture Your Child's Emotional Well-Being

I firmly believe that our children's emotional well-being is just as important as their physical and mental health. After all, emotions play a vital part in their ability to perform tasks and achieve their goals, build meaningful and lasting relationships, and have full and rounded lives. Therefore, as parents, we should also pay attention to the emotional state of our children, so that their emotions don't become a hindrance to their happiness and success. In this subchapter, I've listed four things that you can do to nurture your child's emotional well-being.

Foster a Safe Space for Your Child

The other tips I included in this subchapter will not be useful if your child doesn't feel safe around you. If they have felt misunderstood, judged, or rejected by you, then it's likely that they have already built a wall around their heart to guard their emotions and keep you out. Before you even attempt to nurture your child's emotional well-being, make sure to foster a safe space for them by acknowledging past hurts and apologizing if necessary. Reassure them that you're on their team and that you're going to help them navigate their emotions moving forward. Of course, words aren't enough to make a child feel safe. Your actions must back up your words to make your child feel like they can rely on you.

With that said, whether or not there are past hurts that you need to address, you can foster a safe space for your child by:

- Acknowledging their emotions, tending to their emotional needs, and providing them with emotional support when they're under stress.

- Creating an open line of communication between you and your child—making room for honesty without judgment, and correction without anger.

- Respecting your child's opinions, individuality, and boundaries and not forcing them to open up to you when they're not ready to share their feelings.

Coregulate Your Child's Emotions

Parent training teaches parents effective techniques on how to coregulate their child's emotions during a dysregulated episode. One of these techniques includes emotional modeling, where parents are asked to model behaviors that they want to see in their children (Rosanbalm & Murray, 2017).

To demonstrate, consider this example: Your child is having a dysregulated episode at a busy airport. Strangers are starting to stare, and you're worried that your child may refuse to board the flight if this continues. What do you do?

Some parents may show frustration toward the child, while others may resort to threats, whether intentionally or not, by telling the child that they will leave them at the airport if they don't behave. Sadly, many parents fall back on negative reinforcement when dealing with a stressful situation even though it doesn't accomplish anything but cause more distress to the child.

During a dysregulated episode, your instinct may be to match your child's negative emotions or even overpower them, thinking that they will be subdued if you show greater emotions. However, scolding a child in this situation is not going to help them calm down. In fact, it may even trigger their RSD, which will only worsen their dysregulated episode.

Remember that our job as parents is to always defuse the situation, not aggravate it. Instead of meeting your child at the peak of their emotions, you must use emotional modeling and remain calm, showing no signs of frustration or panic, so that the child can feel reassured that whatever triggered their fight-or-flight response isn't a real threat. Because they don't see you, their provider and protector, reacting negatively, they'll know they're safe from the trigger. Their instinct will tell them to relax. And once the child is calm enough to listen, you may begin other coregulating methods, like guided breathing exercises, until they have completely calmed down.

With that said, you should remember that coregulation is not the same as coddling. If the child did something wrong, it is absolutely necessary to discipline them. The point of emotional modeling is to give them time to collect themselves so they will be more receptive when you correct their behavior in a firm manner. If you attempt to reprimand them while they're still in a dysregulated episode, they won't be able to understand what you're saying because they'll only see your emotions. Seeing you upset will only make them more upset, so trying to discipline them at this point will only be unproductive.

Additionally, here are some questions you can ask your child to help them process their negative feelings:

- Do you need my help or do you just want me to listen?

- Can you tell me why you're upset? (If the child answers "I don't know," you may ask them, "What happened before you cried?" Walk them through the events that directly preceded the episode, but don't push them if they seem uncomfortable.)

- How are you feeling right now? What can I do to help?

Boost Your Child's Self-Esteem

In the previous subchapter, we examined three ways in which ADHD affects an individual's self-esteem, one being poor self-perception in comparison to others. Because of ADHD's impact on a child's cognitive functions, they may think that they are less smart or capable than their peers. To combat this issue, we can teach our children some positive affirmations that they can recite whenever they're feeling bad about themselves or have the urge to compare themselves to others.

For example, one of the first positive affirmations that I taught my twins is: "I am special. I am unique. I am one-of-a-kind." These phrases have taught my children that their unique individualities make them special, and so there is no need for conformity. They don't need to hide their authentic selves because there is nothing wrong with the way they are.

I also love using my twins' strengths as positive affirmations. My girl, for example, is a very creative person. She likes writing stories and poems as well as making arts and crafts. Therefore, I taught her to say, "I am creative. I am talented. My imagination has no bounds." Meanwhile, my boy is a very friendly person. Other kids at their school flock to him because of his kindness and sense of humor. His positive affirmation sounds like, "I am kind. I am funny. I bring joy to others just by being who I am."

Aside from affirmations, positive reinforcements like praise and rewards also boost a child's self-esteem and self-confidence. Tell them that they're doing a good job whenever they perform a desired behavior. If they're showing progress in areas they struggle with, like their academic performance or social skills, even if the progress doesn't meet your expectations, it pays to let them know that you're proud of them. Not only will this boost their self-esteem, but your words of affirmation and encouragement also combat their RSD.

Organize Supervised Playdates

Supervised playdates allow you to monitor your child's ability to socialize with their peers and identify if there are any problems with their social skills. To successfully organize a supervised playdate, here are some tips:

- Don't hover around your child during the playdate. Give them space to freely interact with their peers and intervene only when necessary.

- If your child is isolating themselves, don't force them to play with other kids. Encourage them with positive affirmations, but avoid language that may lead to feelings of guilt or shame and a stronger desire for isolation. For example, "Aren't you lonely being all by yourself?" sends an underlying message that being alone is equivalent to being lonely, which can be harmful to an introverted child's self-esteem.

- Plan various activities that the children can do together. You can prepare a physical activity, a creative activity, and a "sedentary" activity for the playdate. Preparing these different options ensures that the playdate remains stimulating for the children. For example, you can facilitate party games at the beginning of the playdate, since children are likely already excited and "hyped up" to be meeting each other. When they're tired of running around, you can transition to arts and crafts while other parents prepare snacks for the kids. When snacks are ready, the young ones can watch a movie together as they eat. Putting the "sedentary" activity at the end gives them time to cool down. By the time everyone's on the way home, the kids are tired and may even fall asleep during the car ride.

If our goal is to raise happy hyperactive kids, as the title of this book suggests, then we can't ignore the importance of their emotions. The four methods I outlined in this chapter are just some simple examples of how you can nurture their emotional well-being. Like earlier, I highly recommend parent training so you can work closely with a professional and come up with a strategy that meets your goals.

Chapter 4 Review

- Our children's emotional well-being is just as important as their physical and mental health.

- Children with ADHD may suffer from emotion dysregulation, RSD, low self-esteem, and poor social skills because of both neurological impairments and the social stigma surrounding their disorder.

- Parents can nurture their children's emotional well-being by fostering a safe space, practicing emotional coregulation, boosting their child's self-esteem, and organizing supervised playdates.

Chapter 4 Exercise

1. Of the four issues in emotional well-being that we discussed in the first subchapter, identify which ones your child is currently facing. Are they experiencing other issues in this area that need to be addressed?

2. For each suggestion presented in the second section of this chapter, create a specific plan of how you're going to put them in action (e.g. emotion coregulation—guided breathing practice):

   a. Safe space

   b. Emotion coregulation

   c. Self-esteem

   d. Supervised playdates

3. List at least three other methods that you're committed to implement to nurture your child's emotional well-being.

Chapter 5:

Addressing Academic Challenges

Everybody is a genius. But if you judge a fish by its ability to climb a tree, it will live its whole life believing that it is stupid.
–Albert Einstein

Both of my twins have ADHD, but they have different presentations of the disorder. My daughter is the predominantly inattentive type, while my son is the predominantly hyperactive-impulsive type. Although he has trouble sitting still, my boy surprisingly never had any problems at school. He may not be on the honor roll, but his grades have always been consistent.

On the contrary, my daughter's grades are more, let's say, diverse. She has top scores in subjects like math, language, and literature, but her marks suffer in subjects like science, history, and geography. During a parent-teacher conference at their school, her teacher pulled me aside to talk to me about her low grades in these subjects.

"Your daughter seems to be a bright kid. She can solve math problems that are complex for her age. She's also well spoken and has a wide vocabulary," she said, and then, with a frown, she asked, "So why do you think she is struggling in science and the social sciences?"

I smiled and answered her question simply by saying, "ADHD."

Her brows arched and her eyes widened as she nodded. "Ah, that explains it."

Like I've said earlier, the ADHD brain is interest-based. My daughter is good at math, language, and literature because she likes numbers and books. She struggles with science and the social sciences because ADHD affects her working memory. She's also not good in these subjects because, in her own words, the topics are "boring," whereas literary stories are "spellbinding" and mathematical equations are "exhilarating." She only likes to read books that spark her imagination, which is something that the different parts of the cell just can't do.

As you can see from my twins' example, the impact of ADHD on academic performance varies per individual. Therefore, our goal in this chapter is to identify common academic challenges that children with ADHD struggle with, as well as practical steps that we can take to help our children improve their performance at school.

Academic Challenges From ADHD

Standardized curriculums in schools don't cater to interest-based neurodiverse brains, resulting in academic roadblocks for children with ADHD that their neurotypical peers don't normally face. It is not uncommon for individuals with ADHD to struggle in school, especially in subjects they find uninteresting. The academic challenges that children with ADHD face can have significant effects on their self-esteem and their futures. In fact, individuals with ADHD, specifically teen boys, are more likely to fail their classes and to drop out of school than their non-ADHD peers (ADDitude Editors, 2020).

If we want to help our children succeed in school, we must first be aware of the difficulties that may stem from their disorder. In this subchapter, we will answer these questions: How can the main symptoms of ADHD (i.e. inattentiveness, hyperactivity, and impulsivity) affect my child's academic performance? What are hyperfocus and time blindness, and how do they hinder my child at school? What is executive dysfunction and how does it relate to ADHD? Lastly, what learning disorders are common among children with ADHD?

ADHD Symptoms

Inattentiveness can present itself at school in various ways. For some children with ADHD, it means daydreaming during class when they find the topic of discussion or subject uninteresting, making careless mistakes when answering tests or doing assignments, and getting easily distracted during activities where sustained attention is required. Other children with ADHD may find it difficult to follow instructions, stay organized, or finish schoolwork on time.

Just like inattentiveness, hyperactivity and impulsivity also have different presentations at school. A child with ADHD may get up from their seat, run around the room, or talk loudly in the middle of class. They may squirm or fidget in their seat, talk to their classmates, or do similar things that distract other kids from learning. They may answer questions directed at others or give an answer before the teacher even finishes asking. They may also interrupt a classmate who is reciting and get impatient while waiting for their turn.

Hyperfocus

Ashinoff and Abu-Akel (2021) defined hyperfocus as "a phenomenon that reflects one's complete absorption in a task, to a point where a person appears to completely ignore or 'tune out' everything else." Hyperfocus is usually activated when an individual finds a task interesting, or if there is a sense of urgency to complete a task.

Hyperfocus isn't inherently harmful or bad. However, it can be detrimental to a child's academic performance if their brain decides to focus on something other than the task they're supposed to be doing. When hyperfocus is activated, it's like the brain is a plane on auto-pilot mode, and the individual has no control over its destination.

For example, a child may become hyperfocused on their extracurricular activities or hobbies, making it difficult to study for their upcoming exams. By the time their sense of urgency kicks in, they may not have enough time to finish reviewing their lessons. Similarly, they may only want to study certain subjects they're interested in, like my daughter. She can stay focused for hours while solving math problems, but she gets easily distracted when reading about igneous, sedimentary, and metamorphic rocks.

Time Blindness

If you remember from previous chapters, we already discussed how neuroimaging scans show the differences between the ADHD brain and the neurotypical brain. There is weaker function in the prefrontal cortex of the latter, which is the part of the brain responsible for time perception. In particular, the "dorsolateral prefrontal cortex is considered as the region most involved in time perception" (Fontes et al., 2016).

In this regard, ADHD can cause time blindness, which is "the inability to sense when time has passed and estimate the time needed to get something done" (ADDA Editorial Team, 2023b). While this is not an official condition, it has been observed in many individuals with ADHD, causing disruptions in their personal, social, academic, and professional lives.

More specifically, there are five aspects of time perception that are affected by ADHD (ADDA Editorial Team, 2023; Ptacek et al., 2019):

- Time estimation (e.g., "How much time has passed? How much time is needed to complete a task?")

- Time horizon (e.g. "When should I start this task? How much time is left before the task becomes urgent?")

- Time management (e.g., "In what order should I accomplish my tasks? How much time should I spend on each task?")

- Time sequencing (e.g., "When is this event happening? Does it come before or after this other event?")

- Time reproduction (e.g., "I once completed this task in thirty minutes, so why did it take me two hours now?")

These five aspects of time blindness can lead to missed deadlines and appointments, which can be detrimental to one's academic and professional performance. Additionally, people with ADHD are known as serial procrastinators because of time blindness. If the task at hand is uninteresting, they need a sense of urgency to motivate them to get started.

Executive Dysfunction

Before we talk about what executive dysfunction is, let's first define what executive function means. According to Rodden (2021), executive function pertains "to the cognitive and mental abilities that help people engage in goal-directed action." Meanwhile, Sisson (2023) describes it as the ability "to self-regulate, plan for short- and long-term results of their actions, and make necessary adjustments to meet goals."

Executive functions include but are not limited to working memory, processing speed, temporal processing, sustained attention, self-restraint, self-motivation, planning, problem solving, and cognitive switching. However, like many other neurodevelopmental conditions, ADHD affects an individual's cognitive development, function, and processes, leading to executive dysfunction (Coghill et al., 2018; Rodden, 2021; Rubia, 2018).

When a child experiences executive dysfunction, these important brain processes are affected. They are unable to plan, organize, and execute tasks, all of which are important in maintaining good academic standing. Without these abilities, a child may fall behind on their lessons and schoolwork. Executive dysfunction also affects working memory and motivation, which becomes a big issue when they're preparing for exams. Lastly, their ability to restrain themselves is also hindered when executive dysfunction occurs. When this happens, they may choose playing video games over studying for an exam or watching YouTube videos over doing their assignment. The importance and urgency of tasks are overridden by interest because of executive dysfunction.

Because executive dysfunction is hard to detect just by observance, some parents may think that their children are being lazy because they're doing other things when they should be studying. To help you identify executive dysfunction, here are some questions to consider:

- Is your child procrastinating on important and urgent tasks?

- Is your child finding it more difficult to understand, process, and analyze information? Do they often ask you to repeat instructions?

- Is your child more easily distracted than usual?

- Has your child been experiencing more emotionally dysregulated episodes recently? Do they get easily frustrated over minor setbacks and inconveniences?

- Has your child been sluggish? Have they been spacing out more frequently?

- Has your child been more forgetful than usual?

- Does your child have trouble with multitasking? Are they too focused on one task or activity? Or are they switching between tasks without completing any?

- Does your child find it difficult to stick to their schedule or follow through with their plans?

Comorbid Learning Disorders

Even though ADHD and its symptoms can hinder an individual's ability to learn, ADHD is technically not considered a learning disability. However, it often comes with comorbid learning disorders like dyslexia, dysgraphia, and dyscalculia. It is estimated the comorbidity for ADHD and learning disabilities ranges between 31% to 45%. If we look at specific learning disorders, the comorbidity rates vary. Particularly, it is estimated to be 25% to 48% for reading-related learning disorders and ADHD, while it is 11% to 30% for math-related learning disorders and ADHD (Crisci et al., 2021).

Both dyslexia and dysgraphia are related to the processing of words. Dyslexia is a learning disability that hinders reading. Children with dyslexia find it difficult to associate sounds with letters and words, to understand the meaning of words and grammar, and to spell words. Meanwhile, dysgraphia is a learning disability related to writing. Children with dysgraphia may find it difficult to turn their thoughts into written words, hold a writing instrument, and write legibly. Grammar and syntax structure may also be a challenge for them.

Lastly, dyscalculia is a learning disability related to math and problem solving. However, it isn't limited to adding, subtracting, multiplying, and dividing numbers. Dyscalculia also makes it difficult to remember number sequences and leads to a poor sense of direction (National Institute of Neurological Disorders and Stroke [NINDS], 2023; Bailey, 2020).

How to Help Your Child Overcome Academic Challenges

As parents, I think it's only normal for us to have certain expectations regarding our children's academic performance. It may be initially disappointing when our expectations aren't met, but we must remember that our children have a condition that they didn't choose to have and often can't control. It is our responsibility to provide them with the right tools to help them overcome the academic challenges they are facing. In this regard, this subchapter will focus on five solutions to the academic challenges we've discussed.

Fidget Toys

In recent years, I've noticed that fidget toys have become more popular in the mainstream, thanks to social media. However, before they gained popularity, children with ADHD have been using fidget toys to mitigate their symptoms in the short run. In fact, there have been several studies showing the positive impact of non-distracting movement to the academic performance of a child with ADHD. More recently, it has been proven to improve a child's attention in class, especially when performing tasks, as well as decrease the disruptive behaviors they exhibit at school, such as talking to their classmates or looking around the room (Aspiranti & Hulac, 2021).

Positive Reinforcement

If you want to teach a dog how to sit, what do you do? You say the command, show the dog how it's done, and when it follows your command, you offer praise and give it treats, right? By repeating this process, the dog learns the desired behavior. Even if you don't give it treats, it will eventually do as you say.

The process of teaching an individual your desired behavior by giving them rewards and praise is called positive reinforcement. The APA (n.d.e.) defines this as "an increase in the probability of occurrence of some activity because that activity results in the presentation of a stimulus or some circumstance."

Positive reinforcement works on humans, too. For instance, awards and recognition for good grades encourage students to work hard on their studies. Athletes undergo intensive training to win medals. Musicians strive to make good music for the admiration of their fans.

In terms of ADHD, positive reinforcements have also been proven to result in not only reinforcing desired behaviors but also mitigating unwanted behaviors (Bakar & Zainal, 2020; Van der Oord & Tripp, 2020). In simpler words, you can use positive reinforcement to either teach or correct behaviors. By using rewards, you can make important and urgent tasks more interesting, allowing the ADHD brain to shift gears.

Remember, however, that children with ADHD may suffer from time blindness, which can make them feel unmotivated if the desired behavior doesn't immediately reward them. In other words, a future goal leads to a delayed reward, and if there's no reward to be earned now, then there's no motivation for the ADHD brain to start a task.

Therefore, you must make use of short-term positive reinforcements to motivate your child to perform the task now. For example, if their exams are two weeks away, you want to encourage them to start reviewing today. What can you do to motivate your child to study?

For my twins, what I do is I turn their review sessions into a sort of game show where they can win prizes if they answer a given number of questions correctly. The power to choose the dinner menu for the whole week, a chance to be excused from doing chores on the weekend, and 10 minutes added to their screen time before bed are some of the rewards they can earn if they can answer 80% of the questions I ask.

If reading is proving to be difficult because of inattentiveness, I taught my twins to use snacks or candies as a reward. They can eat a piece of their favorite treat (gummy bears for my daughter and sour candies for my son) for every two paragraphs they successfully read.

I also make use of long-term rewards for long-term goals to teach my children the importance of consistency and perseverance. For example, I give monetary rewards to my children if they're able to maintain or improve their grades on their report card. For every grade that stays the same, I give them $5. If they're able to bump up their grade, I give them $10. Therefore, they can earn up to $50 in a term if they do well in their studies.

Of course, positive reinforcement doesn't always lead to the results we expect. You have to keep your child's current abilities, level of executive functioning, and intensity of symptoms at the forefront of your mind. This is why I also reward effort. If I can see that my twins are trying their best, that's enough for me. Let's not limit our children to the letters we see on their report cards. At the end of the day, our main goal is to create better study habits for the long run, so don't be rigid with your standards of success. If needed, make adjustments to your reward system and factor in your child's opinion. What rewards would they prefer? What results can they commit to achieving?

Time Management Tools

There are two time management tools that effectively categorize tasks and identify which ones need to be prioritized. The first one is called the Pareto principle, which states that 20% of the work causes 80% of the results (The Investopedia Team, 2022). To demonstrate, let's say there are 10 steps needed to complete your art project for school. The Pareto principle claims that there are two steps that will lead to 80% of the work being completed. The question is, which of the 10 steps will lead to this result?

Some children with ADHD may find it hard to start a project because they feel overwhelmed by the number of steps needed to complete it. The Pareto principle encourages you to identify and prioritize the tasks that take you as close to the finish line as possible. You override time blindness by identifying which task needs to be done first and how much time can be spent on each. If they are working within a very limited amount of time, it also allows them to submit an almost complete project instead of not being able to submit the project at all.

The second time management tool is called the Eisenhower Matrix. The Eisenhower Matrix categorizes tasks first by level of importance and then by level of urgency. Tasks can be separated into four quadrants: 1) tasks that are both important and urgent, 2) tasks that are urgent but not important, 3) tasks that are important but not urgent, and 4) tasks that are neither important nor urgent (Nevins, 2023).

Your child will complete tasks from the first to the fourth quadrant, making sure to move items in the third quadrant to the first quadrant as they become more urgent. Not only does the Eisenhower Matrix help with time management, but it also targets issues with time horizon and sequencing. If you remember from the previous chapter, these four aspects of time processing answer the questions: "When should I start this task? How much time is left before the task becomes urgent?

When is this event happening? Does it come before or after this other event?"

Assistive Learning Tools

Assistive learning tools turn boring textbooks and slide presentations into more interesting and engaging study materials. There are many different kinds of interactive learning tools that you can utilize. For example, colorful picture flashcards allow children to make associations between words and pictures. You can use this if there are terms they need to memorize in subjects like science, history, and geography. You may also put visual aids on the walls of your child's study area to help them memorize important terms or details.

If you're planning to make assistive learning tools for your child, make sure they are interesting but not distracting. It's okay to have visual aids on the wall, but don't put up so many materials that they become overwhelming for the child. If possible, make them as adaptable to most, if not all, of your child's subjects as well. This allows you to customize the material easily without spending too much time and effort on it. (Remember the parenting tips we discussed in Chapter 3. Don't stretch yourself too thin.)

Alternatively, there are digital tools and applications that aid children with special learning needs, including those with ADHD and learning disabilities. These assistive learning tools include audiobooks, text-to-speech programs, optical character recognition programs, text-predictive software, portable word processors, speech recognition software, talking calculators, and electronic math worksheets (Starkman, 2023). These assistive educational technologies make reading, math, and information processing a lot easier for children with ADHD and learning disabilities.

Special Education and Tutoring Services

In our support group meetings, one of the most frequently asked questions is, "Is ADHD eligible for special education?" Many parents look into special education as a last resort after exhausting all of their efforts to help their child improve their academic performance yet still not achieving their desired results.

In my opinion, unless your child has a comorbid learning disability, a consistent treatment and management strategy is enough to improve their academic performance. By targeting the symptoms that cause academic setbacks and challenges, your child will be able to learn at almost the same pace, if not on equal footing, as their neurotypical peers. They may need assistive learning tools and positive reinforcement to stay focused and motivated, but special education isn't necessary in most cases.

With that said, it doesn't hurt to know your options, right? In the United States, the *Individuals with Disabilities Education Act* (IDEA) and Section 504 of the *Rehabilitation Act of 1973* provide special education services and accommodations to students (CDC, 2023f). Let's discuss each of these options as well as private tutoring.

Special Education (IDEA)

IDEA is a federal law that mandates "free appropriate public education to eligible children with disabilities" (Office for Civil Rights, n.d.a). An individualized educational plan (IEP) is created for a child with special learning needs given that they meet the criteria of eligibility under IDEA. Unfortunately, an ADHD diagnosis doesn't guarantee eligibility unless the child meets the criteria specified in Section 300.8 of this law (Office for Civil Rights, n.d.b).

Other countries have different laws and criteria for eligibility, so I recommend that you do further reading about this topic if you're considering enrolling your child in special education. There are also private special education institutions in and out of the United States that parents can consider. However, like with most private schools, you'll need to prepare for higher tuition and other fees.

504 Plan (Rehabilitation Act)

According to the U.S. Department of Health and Human Services (2006), "Section 504 of the *Rehabilitation Act of 1973* is a national law that protects qualified individuals from discrimination based on their disability." Under Section 504, a 504 plan can be created for a child with special learning needs. The State Council on Developmental Disabilities of California (SCDD, n.d.) defines a 504 plan as "a blueprint or plan for how a child will have access to learning at school" that "provides services and changes to the learning environment to meet the needs of the child as adequately as other students"

A 504 plan will detail the "specific accommodations, supports, or services" needed by the child to learn effectively in class, the provider of each service, and "the person responsible for ensuring the plan is implemented" (SCDD, n.d.). Through this plan, the parents can rest assured that their child receives the assistance they need and that there is accountability if said assistance is not provided by the school. Under the Act, a 504 plan comes at no cost to the parents as it is funded by the federal government (SCDD, n.d.; Office for Civil Rights, 2023).

Private Tutoring

Private tutoring is another great option for children who need additional help with their studies. There are private tutors who also have special certifications in assisting children with neurodevelopmental conditions such as ADHD, ASD, and learning disabilities.

Private tutoring fosters one-on-one interaction between the tutor and the student, whereas a traditional classroom requires a teacher to divide their attention among dozens of students. With such a focused environment, the tutor can create an action plan that caters to your child's problem points and specific learning needs. Private tutors with specialization on children with neurodevelopmental disorders are also well-informed on the symptoms and traits of ADHD that inhibit learning, so they can make the sessions more suitable for your child and more conducive for their learning.

Although private tutoring has the great potential to improve your child's academic performance, it can be a costly option. Don't forget to consider the rates of private tutoring services in your area before making a decision.

And with that, I hope you've found tips on this chapter that you can use to help your child overcome the academic challenges they are currently facing. Our children spend a considerable chunk of their time at school, so it's understandable if their academic performance affects their self-esteem. If a child feels like they're failing and falling behind in comparison to their classmates, they will have a poorer perception of self. But if a child feels like they're succeeding at school, they become happier and more confident individuals.

Chapter 5 Review

- ADHD is not considered a learning disability, although its symptoms may hinder one's ability to learn. ADHD and learning disorders like dyslexia, dysgraphia, and dyscalculia also have significant comorbidity rates.

- ADHD traits like hyperfocus, time blindness, and executive dysfunction may also lead to academic challenges.

- One of the simplest ways to combat the hindrances to learning caused by ADHD symptoms is by giving your child fidget toys.

- To address academic challenges brought by ADHD, parents can use positive reinforcement, time management tools, and interactive learning aids.

- Parents may also consider enrolling their child in special education. In the United States, there are two plans for special education: a 504 plan or an individualized education program (IEP). For those who have the means, private tutoring offers a focused learning environment for children with ADHD.

Chapter 5 Exercise

1. What academic goals do you expect your child to achieve? Is your child's current academic performance above, below, or similar to your expectations?

2. What academic challenges does your child experience, if any? You may list issues that aren't included in this chapter.

3. Make a commitment to meet your child's teachers so you can discuss their performance at school.

4. Given your expectations and assessment, as well as the teachers' feedback on your child's performance, what can you do to address the academic challenges you've identified? Are there tools or suggestions from this chapter that you can implement or utilize?

5. Do some research on special education in your school district. Does your child's current school offer such a program?

Chapter 6:

Celebrating Strengths and Progress

If you can't fly, then run. If you can't crawl, then walk. If you can't walk, then crawl. But whatever you do, you have to keep moving forward.
–Martin Luther King, Jr.

Oftentimes, parents are influenced by an arbitrary set of social rules that become the guideline by which they raise their children. We can see this forced conformity more clearly if we look at the way our parents were raised by our grandparents, how we were raised by our parents, and how we are now raising our children. There are things that parents could do in the past that were socially acceptable. For example, corporal punishment was considered a justifiable form of discipline during our grandparents' time, but it is largely frowned upon and, in many places, illegal in this current age.

Social norms can seep into our perception of our children's abilities. We may have certain expectations of how our children should behave and what achievements they should reach at certain ages. When our children don't meet these expectations, we may feel disappointed or frustrated with them and with ourselves.

Remember neurodiversity? We talked about it in the first chapter. To recap, neurodiversity implores us to change our perspective so that we can view our children's condition not as a disability but simply as a difference. By shifting our mindset, we are able to celebrate our children's strengths and progress without the limitation of social norms.

In previous chapters, we've identified ADHD traits that hinder our children's happiness. Executive dysfunction, emotion dysregulation, RSD, and poor social skills, among others, can lead to low self-esteem, isolation, and overall feelings of dejection. In this chapter, we will focus on things that lead to their happiness—their strengths, interests, and achievements—while setting reasonable milestones that foster progress and growth.

Identify Your Child's Interests

We already know by now that the ADHD brain is interest-based. This is why children with ADHD tend to choose tasks that they find interesting and why they may switch between tasks without finishing any. This also explains why some people may have a rotating cast of interests, like my friend Marie.

Marie has a "hobby corner" in her home. Two tall bookshelves in her living room are filled with puzzles, knitting yarns, miniature model houses, tools for leather making, and other hobbies that she has abandoned over the years. When I asked Marie why she hasn't let go of the items she no longer uses, she said, "I don't know. I may find them interesting again someday!"

There are some people like my friend Marie who jumps from one hobby to another to scratch the itch in her ADHD brain, but there are also people who fixate on one interest, sticking with it for a long time. Often, children with ADHD will hyperfixate on things they like. Hyperfixation is a state of full immersion on an interesting activity. It also involves a heightened and sustained level of focus. When something activates hyperfixation in the ADHD brain, individuals tend to give it more attention than other things in their life (ADDA, 2023b; Flippin, 2023).

Don't be surprised, however, if your child is more like my friend Marie. After all, children are yet to build a strong sense of self, so it's only natural if their interests change rapidly. They'll want to try anything that catches their attention or piques their curiosity, so it is our job as parents to make sure they're pursuing their interests with purpose. To help you identify which of your child's interests are worth pursuing, here are some tips.

- Observe their actions, and consider these questions:

  o What activities have they shown interest in lately? Is there anything in particular they have shown the most interest in?

  o How long have they been interested in this activity?

  o How much time do they spend doing the activity?

  o How does the activity make your child feel?

  o Does the activity have any effect on their symptoms? If yes, does it worsen or improve their symptoms?

- If you've noticed a particular activity they have shown interest in, you may speak to your child about it and ask them what they like about it as well as how they feel about it. You may also ask them to show you how to do said activity or what progress they have made, if any.

- Similarly, whenever your child initiates a conversation about their interest, make sure you pay attention. Learn about your child's interests so you can engage in discussions about them.

- If you notice any changing patterns in the things they're showing interest in, don't limit their curiosity. Like I said earlier, children are bound to have evolving interests as they grow up and get to know themselves better. What's more important is you take note of the interests they keep even while going through these changes.

- Find a role model from whom your child can learn more about their interests. For example, a child who likes art may benefit from speaking to an artist who can show her their techniques, while a kid who likes dinosaurs may enjoy speaking to a paleontologist.

- If your child doesn't show a special interest in any particular activity, perhaps you can encourage them to focus on one of their many interests just to see how they like it.

Once your child finds an interest, they may want to speak about it constantly in an excitable manner, which others may find overzealous or weird. Therefore, one of the best things we can do for our children with ADHD is to raise them in a neurodivergent-affirming environment where their interests are encouraged and where their hyperfixations are not seen or labeled negatively. The tips I've listed in this subchapter will not only help you identify your child's interests, but they will also make your child feel welcomed, loved, and supported.

Nurture Your Child's Strengths

As your child tries new things and explores their interests, you will begin to observe certain skills and talents that they possess. When your child starts to show these strengths, it's time to hone in on the interests that brought these skills and talents to the surface. Let me tell you a story.

Jade, a fellow mom in my support group, was diagnosed with ADHD when she was 14 years old. She describes her symptoms as a blessing and a superpower, not a curse. She said that her interest-based brain has led her to become the person she was always meant to be.

"I was the only child, the only successor, in a family of doctors. Three generations on both sides of the family went into the medical field, and my paternal grandparents founded a small clinic in Ohio in the 1960s. By all measures, my path was chosen for me before I was even born. I was meant to study medicine, just as my parents and their parents, and my grandparents' parents had. I was going to be a doctor. But at a very young age, my inclination has always been toward the arts. I liked painting. I liked sculpting with clay. I liked making weird things out of ordinary things. As much as I liked touching paint and clay and glue and glitter, I disliked touching other people, which apparently is a prerequisite in medicine." She laughed. "I knew from a young age that I wasn't going to be a doctor. I was always meant to be an artist."

Luckily, her parents didn't stop her from pursuing her interests, and they became even more encouraging when they saw that she had a talent. "They enrolled me in art classes. They introduced me to some of their friends who collected art. They brought me to museums, galleries, art fairs... Because I had the support of my parents, I didn't have a sliver of a doubt that I wanted to pursue the arts. I believed in myself because they believed in me."

Today, Jade owns a pottery studio in our area. Not only does she make the most beautiful bespoke ceramics, but she also teaches others who are interested in her craft.

And what became of her grandparents' clinic in Ohio? Well, her parents still run it with a small team of doctors. They're still clinging onto hope that one of Jade's three children will want to be a doctor so they can pass on their legacy to their kin, and Jade's eldest seems to show promise!

Although Jade's interest in the arts was not what her parents had expected, they still encouraged her to pursue it. Without their support, she probably would have still become an artist as an adult, but the fact that they were on her side from the beginning gave her confidence. She faced fewer obstacles on her path to her dreams because her parents allowed her to be herself.

From Jade's story, we see clearly the impact that we can have as parents on our children's lives. If we nurture their strengths, we boost their self-esteem. We allow them an opportunity to sharpen their skills and talents at a young age, giving them more time to master their interests. Even if they decide to change their path one day, they will still carry with them the confidence that we have equipped them with, so they can overcome whatever obstacles they may face on the way to their dreams.

Depending on your child's strengths, there are a multitude of ways in which you can nurture them. Here are some examples:

- With work and household expenses, it's only understandable that you won't have the time or funds to encourage all of your child's interests, so allocate most of your resources to wherever they show the most potential. Not only are you able to save resources, but your child is also more likely to gain mastery if they develop their skills and talents in one area.

- Jade's parents enrolled her in different art classes as she was growing up. She had classes in sketching, painting, pottery, sculpting, and even metal working. You may also enroll your child in special classes that are related to their area of interest. Your child will be able to hone their skills and talents if they learn from someone who is knowledgeable enough about their interest to coach them toward progress.

- Positive reinforcement also works well to boost a child's self-esteem, just like we discussed in the previous chapter. Acknowledge their strengths and give them recognition when they show progress in their chosen pursuits. If your child is struggling or showing little to no progress, yet they still want to continue with the interest they have chosen, you should also recognize their perseverance.

- Offer constructive criticism. Instead of vague praises, point out specific areas that impressed you. You may also mention areas where they can still improve. However, remember to frame negative feedback in an empathetic way. Here are some examples:

  o "This artwork is amazing!" → "Your brushstrokes are so clean, and the colors you used work so well together! The shading adds depth to your painting, too."

  o "Great job on the game today, bud." → "The shot you made during the fourth quarter of the game was awesome, bud. The way you broke through the other team's defensive play was impressive."

  o "This mistake could have been easily avoided if you were more careful." → "You scored higher in this test than the last one. Good job, sweetie! I'm sure you'll do better again in the next test. Don't forget to double check your solutions so you don't make the same mistakes, okay?"

- Lastly, teach your child to develop self-awareness so they can identify their own strengths and weaknesses. You can do this by asking them these questions:
    - What do you like most about (the interest)?
    - Do you think there's an area where you can still improve?
    - Is there something you're proud of?
    - Is there something you're frustrated with?
    - Are you enjoying what you're doing?
    - What excites you the most about it?

Set Reasonable Milestones

In Chapter 3, we talked about the importance of setting realistic goals for ourselves and our children, but we focused more on its impact on our health and ability to parent. From the perspective of our children's success, happiness, and overall well-being, the importance of setting reasonable milestones cannot be understated.

We need to remember that many children with ADHD often have developmental delays, so we shouldn't measure their progress by comparing them to their neurotypical peers. Doing so will be harmful to the child's self-perception, which will affect their self-esteem.

Instead of seeking external measures of progress, I think it's better to teach our children to look inwardly in search of purpose. Here are some questions you can ask them:

- What do you want to achieve? Do you have goals?

- Some children may give "silly" answers to these questions simply because they're too young to look too far ahead into the future and have long-term plans for themselves. If this is the case, don't focus too much on what their answer is but what it implies. Does your child's answer show creativity? Does it highlight their sense of humor? Does it reveal wisdom beyond their years?

- Why do you want to achieve this goal?

  - This question can reveal your child's purpose, their driving force. For instance, an answer such as "I want to help others" shows that a child is empathetic, while an answer like "I want to travel in space and see aliens" shows curiosity. Their answer will tell us what kind of approach we need to take to help them achieve their goals.

- How do we get to your goal?

  - Dividing a goal into smaller and more manageable steps shows the child a clearer path towards their goal. It also combats the issue of time blindness that prevents a child with ADHD from planning ahead. The steps you come up with together can be the basis of their milestones.

Before we move onto the last part of this chapter, let me leave you with a reminder: As your child grows up, their goals and priorities will change. It is not our job as parents to keep them on the same path while they're experiencing these transitions in their lives. We don't say, "Hey, you wanted to be a pilot when you were five years old. You should keep chasing that dream!" After all, their life is their journey to take, so they get to choose the destination.

Our role in their lives is to act like guides who will show them the best path forward: "This path is too rocky. This one's too steep. This one is long, but the scenery is beautiful if you take it." We're further ahead in terms of life experience—we've already trudged down similar paths, so to speak—so we have the wisdom to show them the way.

"Alexis, what if they don't know what their destination is? What happens then?" Well, go back to the first two things we discussed in this chapter. Help them find their interests and nurture their strengths, and their destination will become clearer.

Celebrate Progress

Throughout this book, we've talked extensively about the hurdles that children with ADHD may face because of their condition. They are disadvantaged in a world that isn't built for them or their needs, and they may even experience judgment from others as a result of the social stigma surrounding neurodiversity. Living in such a world, it's easy for our children to feel discouraged if we don't foster a home that celebrates them for who they are. Without a positive environment to grow up in, their self-perception may become influenced or thwarted by external opinions. They may even think that their differences make them less than others.

Although our children may not always meet the expectations and milestones that others impose upon them, they need to know that their effort and perseverance are appreciated—that their hard work and willingness to improve are more important than external validation.

This is why I say celebrate progress, not achievements, because the latter often hinges upon social norms that are already discriminatory against people with neurodiverse conditions. Graduating with honors, for example, is an achievement in a neurotypical society, but ADHD can hinder a child's ability to learn. Instead of focusing on the final product, the grades, why don't we look at the journey and see where effort was made? Recognize whenever there is an attempt to overcome challenges and celebrate the progress that resulted from this effort.

It's also possible that grades aren't a good measurement of success for a child who has non-academic goals and interests. An athlete's performance at their sport or a dancer's performance on stage is surely more important than what grades they get at school, right? I'm not suggesting that school isn't important for these children, but surely it isn't the only indicator of success. In other words, let us, as parents, recognize wherever progress is made and cultivate an environment where differences are celebrated.

Society tells us that there are certain milestones that a person should reach at certain stages of their life—my kids taught me that life is way more than that. Because my children's happiness and well-being are more important to me than what society thinks, in our house, we make our own rules. I hope that you can make your own rules in your house, too.

Chapter 6 Review

- Some ADHD traits can lead to low self-esteem, isolation, and overall feelings of dejection.

- To raise happy children, we should identify their interests, nurture their strengths, set reasonable milestones, and celebrate their progress.

- Children with ADHD have an interest-based brain, so it's natural for them to have changing interests. Our job as parents is to help identify which interests are worth pursuing.

- When we nurture our children's strengths, we boost their self-esteem and encourage them to master their skills and talents. We can do this by allocating our resources to the area of interest where they show the most potential, enrolling them in special classes, using positive reinforcement, offering constructive criticism, and helping them develop self-awareness.

- Reasonable milestones can be set if we value our children's opinion about the direction they want to take in their lives. We are not here to choose a destination for our child. Instead, let's act like guides that will show them the best path toward their desired destination.

- Achievements are often dictated by existing social norms. To acknowledge our children's differences, let's recognize their effort and celebrate the progress that resulted from it.

Chapter 6 Exercise

1. What are your child's interests? Is there something worth pursuing? What can you do to encourage their interests?

2. What are your child's strengths? Do they have remarkable skills and talents? What can you do to hone them?

3. What milestones has your child already achieved? Based on their current performance and progress, what reasonable milestones can you set for them for the short term? What about for the next year? For the next five years?

4. What kind of progress has your child shown recently? Are there obstacles they have overcome? Are there goals you didn't think they would achieve but did?

5. What steps can you take to ensure that they continue on an upward trajectory?

Conclusion

There are only two lasting bequests we can hope to give our children. One of these is roots, the other, wings.
–John Wolfgang von Goethe

Throughout this book, we found multiple ways to raise happy ADHD kids, but what about the future? What awaits them as they grow older and transition from their childhood to their adolescence? From their adolescence to their adulthood?

Before we answer these questions, let me tell you a story. There is a member in my support group, a 42-year-old father to two kids, aged ten and four, who was diagnosed with ADHD when he was just eight years old. He joined the support group a few months ago, after his oldest son was also diagnosed with the disorder. At first glance, Michael did not look like he had ADHD. He could sit still and pay attention for a long time during meetings—he didn't even fidget or squirm and always responded thoughtfully when other parents asked him questions about growing up with ADHD.

Another member, Darren, a 29-year-old father to an eight-year-old boy with ADHD, received his diagnosis just recently. It happened because as his son was in the process of being diagnosed, the therapist noticed that Darren showed external symptoms of ADHD, too. She advised him to see a colleague of hers, who formally diagnosed him with ADHD at the age of 28.

Michael is a senior partner at a big law firm. He has always been a good student and passed the bar on his first try. Meanwhile, Darren dropped out of college because of poor grades. He started doing odd jobs, like bartending and delivering packages, to support himself until he met his wife. She got pregnant a year into dating, so Darren decided to find a more stable source of income. With his love of food, he decided to start a food truck business with his best friend, which they have now turned into a small restaurant.

I'm telling you these stories to demonstrate the importance of early diagnosis, treatment, and management when it comes to ADHD. While both Michael and Darren—not their real names—ended up doing what they loved in the end, one followed a straighter path toward his dream. Michael was diagnosed at eight years old and received the proper tools to focus in school. Having effective coping strategies at such a young age allowed him to build healthy habits and routines that helped him get through law school, pass the bar exam, and succeed at his job.

On the contrary, Darren's symptoms were ignored or unnoticed in his youth, so he struggled to find his footing as an adult. In our meetings, Darren would tell stories about being extremely impulsive when he was younger, to the point where he would often make risky decisions. His wife's pregnancy, for example, was unplanned. Although there's nothing he loves more than his family, he admitted that they were too young and unprepared to have a baby when they did.

"If I could go back, I won't change anything," Darren told me in a conversation that he generously allowed me to share in this book. He added, "Of course, it would have been nice to know that I had ADHD earlier in life. I didn't do well back in school, and I used to compare myself to my classmates, thinking I was dumb. Why can't I keep up? Why am I always failing my tests? Why am I a failure? Not knowing that I had ADHD took a toll on me. I had low self-esteem in my adolescence. I feel bad for that kid, looking back."

ADHD can have severe consequences in an individual's adolescence and adulthood if left undiagnosed, untreated, and unmanaged. Growing responsibilities, physical changes, and social demands can compound the existing ADHD symptoms. Therefore, it is imperative that we prepare our children as early as possible, so they can avoid unnecessary challenges as they grow up.

Untreated and unmanaged ADHD in adolescence can take the form of risky behaviors, such as of speeding, drunk driving, and unprotected sex, as well as higher dropout rates (Daffner et al., 2022; Margherio et al., 2020; McCarthy, 2019). Meanwhile, in adulthood, ADHD leads to higher unemployment rates and lower income, as well as compulsive buying behaviors (Brook et al., 2015; Jangmo et al., 2021). Can you imagine being an adult who can't keep a job yet spends money impulsively? If we don't teach our children healthy coping mechanisms now, this might just be their reality.

This isn't to say that our children will no longer face challenges in the future if we start preparing them today. Of course, there is no way for us to predict the future. We can't think of every possibility and attempt to solve problems that haven't happened yet. To do so would push us into hypervigilant mode, which we already know is not good for anyone.

As we end the journey we've shared throughout this book, I want to remind you of the advice that Mrs. Hawthorne imparted to me all those years ago: "You don't need to know everything now. The road ahead of you may seem intimidating from where you stand, but you still have plenty of time to learn how to best navigate it. Just do the very best you can every single day."

My dear friend, thank you for joining me in this journey. Your child is lucky to have a parent like you who cares a lot about their happiness and well-being. The future may seem daunting from where you stand, but as long as you do your best every day, that is enough.

Thank you for reading this book and taking steps to achieve your personal goals. I hope you can successfully apply the suggestions and advice included here to your life as I have done to mine.

*Many readers are unaware of how critical **reviews** are to an author or how difficult they are to come by after purchasing a book.*

I would be so grateful if you could write a brief review of Amazon. You can also direct me with thoughts, questions, or suggestions at **www.creativeworksbooks.com**.

I appreciate feedback and read all emails sent to me.

Be sure to check out my other self-help books, workbooks, and coloring books for further exercises and relaxing personal growth tools.

Alexis

About the Author

Alexis Carter has a master's degree and a specialty in behavioral and forensic psychology. Her expertise is in developing positive parenting skill, ADHD self-awareness, healthy relationship strategies, and recognizing negative patterns and self-esteem issues that can lead to unwanted dysfunction in dating, relationships, and in personal and professional lives.

Alexis's goal is to arm teens, men, and women, with practical strategies and techniques to understand ingrained behaviors, develop healthy relationships, create realistic perspectives and priorities, and manage challenges and traumas that can affect personal success.

She has created a library of self-help titles, workbooks journals, and coloring books designed to address self-esteem, coping strategies, stress management, build confidence, and develop mindfulness.

She is excited to add *Hyperactive Happiness* as the first book in her Parenting Success series of books.

When Alexis is not helping others, she is a busy single mom of twins and lives in California with her children.

You can find more of her books on Amazon by visiting

www.amazon.com/stores/Alexis-Carter/author/B0BNH9SB5M

The link to other books in the Doormat series are:

www.amazon.com/dp/B0CKYNHTZT

www.amazon.com/dp/B0BT14QHM9

www.amazon.com/dp/B0BW32CWN9

www.amazon.com/dp/B0BT6V58P4

References

110 best friendship quotes for kids. (n.d.). Lil Tigers. https://www.liltigers.net/friendship-quotes-for-kids/

ADDA Editorial Team. (2023, October 2). *ADHD time blindness: How to detect it and regain control over time.* Attention Deficit Disorder Association. https://add.org/adhd-time-blindness/

ADDA Editorial Team. (2023, March 20). *ADHD & hyperfixation: The phenomenon of extreme focus.* Attention Deficit Disorder Association. https://add.org/adhd-hyperfixation/

ADDitude Editors. (202, April 6). ADHD statistics: New ADD facts and research. *ADDitude.* https://www.additudemag.com/statistics-of-adhd/

ADDitude Editors. (2023, April 15). Your day is getting better—starting now. *ADDitude.* https://www.additudemag.com/slideshows/adhd-famous-quotes-for-a-bad-day/

ADDitude Editors. (2023a, April 28). Bullying is the norm. So is an inadequate response. *ADDitude.* https://www.additudemag.com/bullying-in-schools-adhd-neurodivergent-stude nts-report/

ADDitude Editors. (2023b, October 2). Famous people with ADHD. *ADDitude.* https://www.additudemag.com/slideshows/famous-people-with-adhd/

Ahmad, T.A. (2019, May 20). Meet the Lebanese woman who lost her sight when she was seven, and now empowers the blind to see. *Arab News.* https://www.arabnews.com/node/1499381/lifestyle

American Psychiatric Association. (2023). *Diagnostic and Statistical Manual of Mental Disorders (DSM-5-TR).* https://www.psychiatry.org/psychiatrists/practice/dsm

American Psychological Association. [APA]. (2020, March 4). *Working out boosts brain health.* https://www.apa.org/topics/exercise-fitness/stress

American Psychological Association [APA]. (n.d.a). *Cognitive behavior therapy (CBT)*. APA Dictionary of Psychology. https://dictionary.apa.org/cognitive-behavior-therapy

American Psychological Association [APA]. (n.d.b). *Pharmacotherapy*. APA Dictionary of Psychology. https://dictionary.apa.org/pharmacotherapy

American Psychological Association [APA]. (n.d.c). *Hypervigilance*. APA Dictionary of Psychology. https://dictionary.apa.org/hypervigilance

American Psychological Association [APA]. (n.d.d). *Stress*. APA Dictionary of Psychology. https://dictionary.apa.org/stress

Americans with Disabilities Act 1990 (USA)

Ashinoff, B.K. & Abu-Akel, A. (2021). Hyperfocus: The forgotten frontier of attention. *Psychological Research, 85*(1), pp. 1-19. https://doi.org/10.1007/s00426-019-01245-8

Asking for help quotes. (n.d.). AZ Quotes. https://www.azquotes.com/quotes/topics/asking-for-help.html

Aspiranti, K.B. & Hulac, D.M. (2022). Using fidget spinners to improve on-task classroom behavior for students with ADHD. *Behavioral Analysis in Practice, 15*(2), pp. 454-465. https://doi.org/10.1007/s40617-021-00588-2

Babinski, D.E., Kujawa, A., Kessel, E.M., Arfer, K.B., & Klein, D.N. (2023). Sensitivity to peer feedback in young adolescents with symptoms of ADHD: Examination of neurophysiological self-report measures. *Journal of Abnormal Child Psychology, 47*, pp. 605-617. https://doi.org/10.1007/s10802-018-0470-2

Bailey, E. (2020, February 28). Learning disabilities overview: Reading, writing and math disorders. *ADDitude*. https://www.additudemag.com/slideshows/types-of-learning-disabilities-overview/

Bakar, N. & Zainal, M.S. (2020). The effects of using positive reinforcement techniques to reduce disruptive behavior of pupils with ADHD. *Global Conferences Series: Social Sciences Education and Humanities, 4*. https://series.gci.or.id/article/265/15/icsar-2020-2020

Baumer, N. & Frueh, J. (2021). *What is neurodiversity?* Harvard Health Publishing, Harvard Medical School. https://www.health.harvard.edu/blog/what-is-neurodiversity-202111232645

Brook, J.S., Zhang, C., Brook, D.W., & Leukefeld, C.G. (2015). Compulsive buying: Earlier illicit drug use, impulse buying, depression, and adult ADHD symptoms. *Psychiatry Research, 228*(3), pp. 312-317. https://doi.org/10.1016/j.psychres.2015.05.095

Bustinza, C.C. Adams, R.E., Claussen, A.H., Vitucci, D., Danielson, M.L., Holbrook, J.R., Charania, S.N., Yamamoto, K., Nidey, N., & Froehlich, T.E. (2022). Factors associated with bullying victimization and bullying perpetration in children and adolescents with ADHD: 2016 to 2017 national survey of children's health. *Journal of Attention Disorders, 26*(12), pp. 1535-1548. https://doi.org/10.1177/10870547221085502

Carr, A.W., Bean, R.A., & Nelson, K.F. (2020). Childhood attention-deficit hyperactivity disorder: Family therapy from an attachment based perspective. *Children and Youth Services Review, 119.* https://doi.org/10.1016/j.childyouth.2020.105666.

Caye, A., Spadini, A.V., Karam, R.G., Grevet, E.H., Rovaris, D.L., Bau, C.H.D., Rhode, L.A., & Kieling, C. (2016). Predictors of persistence of ADHD in adulthood: A systematic review of the literature and meta-analysis. *European Child and Adolescent Psychiatry, 25*(11), pp. 1151-1159. https://doi.org/0.1007/s00787-016-0831-8

Centers for Disease Control and Prevention [CDC]. (2022a, August 9). *What is ADHD?* https://www.cdc.gov/ncbddd/adhd/facts.html

Centers for Disease Control and Prevention [CDC]. (2022b, August 9). *Data and statistics.* https://www.cdc.gov/ncbddd/adhd/data.html

Centers for Disease Control and Prevention [CDC]. (2022c, August 9). *Symptoms and diagnosis.* https://www.cdc.gov/ncbddd/adhd/diagnosis.html#ref

Centers for Disease Control and Prevention [CDC]. (2023a, June 6). *3 years.* https://www.cdc.gov/ncbddd/actearly/milestones/milestones-3yr.html

Centers for Disease Control and Prevention [CDC]. (2023b, June 6). *4 years*. https://www.cdc.gov/ncbddd/actearly/milestones/milestones-4yr.html

Centers for Disease Control and Prevention [CDC]. (2023c, June 6). *5 years*. https://www.cdc.gov/ncbddd/actearly/milestones/milestones-5yr.html

Centers for Disease Control and Prevention [CDC]. (2023d, September 27). *Parent training*. https://www.cdc.gov/ncbddd/adhd/behavior-therapy.html

Centers for Disease Control and Prevention [CDC]. (2023e, September 27). *Other concerns and conditions*. https://www.cdc.gov/ncbddd/adhd/conditions.html

Centers for Disease Control and Prevention [CDC]. (2023f, September 27). *School*. https://www.cdc.gov/ncbddd/adhd/school-success.html

Chen, M.H., Lin, H.M., Sue, Y.R., Yu, Y.C., & Yeh, P.Y. (2023). Meta-analysis reveals a reduced surface area of the amygdala in individuals with attention deficit/hyperactivity disorder. *Psychophysiology, 60*(9). https://doi.org/10.1111/psyp.14308

Children and Adults with Attention-Deficit/Hyperactivity Disorder [CHADD]. (2021, February 18). *How the gender gap leaves girls and women undertreated for ADHD*. https://chadd.org/adhd-news/adhd-news-adults/how-the-gender-gap-leaves-girls-and-women-undertreated-for-adhd/

Ciesielski, H. A., Loren, R. E. A., & Tamm, L. (2020). Behavioral Parent Training for ADHD Reduces Situational Severity of Child Noncompliance and Related Parental Stress. Journal of Attention Disorders, 24(5), 758-767. https://doi.org/10.1177/1087054719843181

Coghill, D.R., Banaschewski, T., Bliss, C., Robertson, B. & Zuddas, A. (2018). Cognitive function of children and adolescents with attention-deficit/hyperactivity disorder in a 2-year open-label study of lisdexamfetamine dimesylate. *CNS Drugs, 32*(1), pp. 85-95. https://doi.org/ 10.1007/s40263-017-0487-z

Cleveland Clinic. (2022, October 6). *ADHD medication.* https://my.clevelandclinic.org/health/treatments/11766-adhd-medication

Cleveland Clinic. (2023, March 5). *SNRIs (serotonin and norepinephrine reuptake inhibitors).* https://my.clevelandclinic.org/health/treatments/24797-snri

Community quotes. (n.d.). Brainy Quote. https://www.brainyquote.com/topics/community-quotes

Crisci, G., Caviola, S., Cardillo, C., & Mammarella, I.C. (2021). Executive functions in neurodevelopmental disorders: Comorbidity overlaps between attention deficit and hyperactivity disorder and specific learning disorders. *Frontiers in Human Neuroscience, 15.* https://doi.org/10.3389/fnhum.2021.594234

Daffner, M.S., DuPaul, G.J., Anastopoulos, A.D., & Weyandt, L.L. (2022). From orientation to graduation: Predictors of academic success for freshmen with ADHD. *Journal of Postsecondary Education and Disability, 35*(2), pp. 113-130. https://files.eric.ed.gov/fulltext/EJ1364187.pdf

Daniel, A. (2023, May 13). *She's a UN disability advocate who won't see her own blindness as a disability.* NPR. https://www.npr.org/sections/goatsandsoda/2023/05/13/1174089463/when-getty-began-losing-her-vision-as-a-girl-she-was-told-her-life-was-over-wron

Davydovskaya, Y. (2019, September 11). Mydayis (mixed amphetamine salts). *Medical News Today.* https://www.medicalnewstoday.com/articles/326412#_noHeaderPrefixedContent

Di Lorenzi, R., Balducci, J., Poppi, C., Arcolin, E., Cutino, A., Ferri, P., D'Amico, R., & Filippini, T. (2021). Children and adolescents with ADHD followed up to adulthood: A systematic review of long-term outcomes. *Acta Neuropsychiatrica, 33*(6), pp. 283, 298. https://doi.org/10.1017/neu.2021.23

Dodson, W. (2023, October 11). New insights into rejection sensitive dysphoria. *ADDitude.* https://www.additudemag.com/rejection-sensitive-dysphoria-adhd-emotional-dysregulation/

Empowerment Through Integration. (n.d.). *History.* https://www.etivision.org/history

Ewan, L. (2023, January 25). *What is rejection sensitive dysphoria?* Psycom. https://www.psycom.net/adhd/rejection-sensitive-dysphoria

Fairbank, R. (2023). An ADHD diagnosis in adulthood comes with challenges and benefits. *Monitor in Psychology, 54*(2), p. 52. https://www.apa.org/monitor/2023/03/adult-adhd-diagnosis.

Faraone, S.V. (2018). The pharmacology of amphetamine and methylphenidate: Relevance to neurobiology of attention-deficit/hyperactivity disorder and other psychiatric comorbidities. *Neuroscience & Biobehavioral Reviews, 87*, pp. 255-270. https://doi.org/10.1016/j.neubiorev.2018.02.001

Flippin, R. (2023, August 25). Hyperfocus: The ADHD phenomenon of intense fixation. *ADDitude.* https://www.additudemag.com/understanding-adhd-hyperfocus/

Fogler, J.M., Weaver, A.L., Katusic, S., Voigt, R.G., & Barbaresi, W.J. (2020). Recalled experiences of bullying and victimization in a longitudinal, population-based birth cohort: The influence of ADHD and co-occurring psychiatric disorder. *Journal of Attention Disorders, 26*(1), pp. 15-24. https://doi.org/10.1177/108705472096998

Fontes, R., Ribeiro, J., Gupta, D.S., Machado, D., Lopes-Júnior, F., Magalhães, F., Bastos, V.H., Rocha, K., Marinho, V., Lima, G., Velasques, B., Ribeiro, P., Orsini, M., Pessoa, B., Leite, M.A.A., & Teixeira, S. (2016). Time perception mechanisms at central nervous system. *Neurology International, 8*(1). https://doi.org/10.4081/ni.2016.5939

Food and Drug Administration [FDA]. (2023, August 17). *Prescription stimulant medications.* https://www.fda.gov/drugs/information-drug-class/prescription-stimulant-medications

Friesen, K. & Markowsky, A. (2021). The diagnosis management of anxiety in adolescents with comorbid ADHD. *The Journal of Nurse Practitioners, 17*(1), pp. 65-69. https://doi.org/10.1016/j.nurpra.2020.08.014

Gillespie, C. (2023, June 21). *For most children, ADHD continues into adulthood, study finds.* Very Well Family. https://www.verywellfamily.com/adhd-continues-into-adulthood-for-most-children-study-finds-5199788

Grant, S. (2015, February). Hypervigilant parenting may be harmful to your health. *Attention Magazine,* pp. 18-21. https://d393uh8gb46l22.cloudfront.net/wp-content/uploads/2018/06/ATTN_02_15_HypervigiliantParenting.pdf

Hammer, C. (2023, April 25). Where the hunter-gatherer theory of ADHD breaks down. *ADDitude.* https://www.additudemag.com/hunter-gatherer-theory-adhd-marriage/

Horan, K.S. (2021, December 31). 7 ways ADHD can be seen in the brain. *Psychology Today,* https://www.psychologytoday.com/us/blog/the-reality-of-gen-z/202112/7-ways-adhd-can-be-seen-in-the-brain

Jangmo, A., Kuja-Halkola, R., Pérez-Vigil, A. Almqvist, C., Bulik, C.M., D'Onofrio, B., Lichtenstein, P., Werner-Kiechle, T., & Larsson, H. (2021). Attention-deficit/hyperactivity disorder and occupational outcomes: The role of educational attainment, comorbid developmental disorders, and intellectual disability. *PLoS One, 16*(3). https://doi.org/10.1371/journal.pone.0247724

Johns Hopkins Medicine. (n.d.a). *Attention-deficit/hyperactivity disorder (ADHD) in children.* https://www.hopkinsmedicine.org/health/conditions-and-diseases/adhdadd

John M. Gottman quotes. (n.d.). GoodReads. https://www.goodreads.com/author/quotes/14734208.John_M_Gottman

Junttila, M., Kielinen, M., Jussila, K., Joskitt, L., Mäntymaa, M., Ebeling, H., & Mattila, M.L. (2023). The traits of Autism Spectrum Disorder and bullying victimization in an epidemiological population. *European Child & Adolescent Psychiatry.* https://doi.org/10.1007/s00787-023-02228-2

Khan, S. (2021, October 21). *How do selective norepinephrine reuptake inhibitors work?* RxList.

https://rxlist.com/selective_norepinephrine_reuptake_inhibitors/dr
ug-class.htm

Kingsley, E. & Connolly, M. (2023, June 5). Why ADHD in girls is often overlooked. *ADDitude.* https://www.additudemag.com/the-truth-about-girls-adhd/

León-Barriera, R., Ortegon, R.S., Modesto-Lowe, V., & Chaplin, M.M. (2022). Treating ADHD and comorbid anxiety in children: A guide for clinical practice. *Clinical Pediatrics, 62*(1), pp. 39-46. https://doi.org/10.1177/00099228221111246

Liao, S. (2017, May 10). *Why are ADHD medicines controlled substances?* WebMD. https://www.webmd.com/add-adhd/features/adhd-medicines-controlled-substances

Lovering, N. (2022, February 21). *Can cognitive behavioral therapy help treat ADHD?* PsychCentral. https://psychcentral.com/adhd/cbt-for-adhd

Lu, S., Wei, F., & Li, G. (2021). The evolution of the concept of stress and the framework of the stress system. *Cell Stress, 5*(6), pp. 76-85. https://doi.org/10.15698/cst2021.06.250

Lutz, A.S.F. (2023, June 26). An interview with neurodiversity originator Judy Singer. *Psychology Today.* https://www.psychologytoday.com/intl/blog/inspectrum/202306/an-interview-with-neurodiversity-originator-judy-singer

Margherio, S.M., Capps, R.E., Monopoli, W.J., Evans, S.W., Hernandez-Rodriguez, M., Owens, J.S., & DuPaul, G.J. (2020). Romantic relationships and sexual behavior among adolescents with ADHD. *Journal of Attention Disorders, 25*(10). https://doi.org/10.1177/1087054720914371

Mayo Clinic Staff. (2019, June 15). *Attention-deficit/hyperactivity disorder (ADHD) in children.* Mayo Clinic. https://www.mayoclinic.org/diseases-conditions/adhd/diagnosis-treatment/drc-20350895

Mazzeschi, C., Burrata, L., Germani, A., Cavallina, C., Ghignoni, R., Margheriti, M., & Pazzagli, C. (2019). Parental reflective functioning in mothers and fathers of children with ADHD: Issues regarding assessment and implications for intervention. *Frontiers in Public Health, 7.* https://doi.org/10.3389/fpubh.2019.00263

McCarthy, C. (2019, August 30). *Driving for teens with ADHD: What parents need to know.* Harvard Health Publishing. https://www.health.harvard.edu/blog/teens-with-adhd-and-driving-what-parents-need-to-know-2019083017633

Mehren, A., Reichert, M., Coghill, D., Müller, H.H.O., Braun, N., & Philipsen, A. (2020). Physical exercise in attention deficit hyperactivity disorder—evidence and implications for the treatment of borderline personality disorder. *Borderline Personality Disorder and Emotion Dysregulatio, 7*(1). https://doi.org/10.1186/s40479-019-0115-2

Miller, C. (2023a, April 21). *What is neurodiversity?* Child Mind Institute. https://childmind.org/article/what-is-neurodiversity/

Miller, C. (2023b, January 26). *What are nonstimulant medications for ADHD?* Child Mind Institute. https://childmind.org/article/what-are-nonstimulant-medications-for-adhd/

Minde, K., Roy, J., Bezonsky, R., & Hashemi A. (2010). The effectiveness of CBT in 3-7 year old anxious children: Preliminary data. *Journal of the Canadian Academy of Child and Adolescent Psychiatry, 19*(2), pp. 109-115. https://www.ncbi.nlm.nih.gov/pmc/articles/PMC2868557/

Murray, A.L., Zych, I., Ribeaud, D., & Eisner, M. (2020). Developmental relations between ADHD symptoms and bullying perpetration and victimization in adolescence. *Aggressive Behavior, 47*(1), pp. 58-68. https://doi.org/10.1002/ab.21930

Musa, R.B. & Shafiee, Z. (2007). Depressive, anxiety and stress levels among mothers of ADHD children and their relationships to ADHD symptoms. *ASEAN Journal of Psychiatry, 8*(1), p. 20-28. https://www.researchgate.net/publication/281856931

National Children's Bureau. (2023). *Bullying and Autism: Developing Effective Anti-Bullying Practice.* Anti-Bullying Alliance. https://anti-bullyingalliance.org.uk/sites/default/files/uploads/attachments/Autism%20and%20bullying%20guide%202023_FINAL.pdf

National Health Service [NHS]. (2021a, December 24). *Causes: Attention deficit hyperactivity disorder (ADHD).*

https://www.nhs.uk/conditions/attention-deficit-hyperactivity-disorder-adhd/causes/

National Health Service [NHS]. (2021b, December 24). *Overview: Attention deficit hyperactivity disorder (ADHD)*. https://www.nhs.uk/conditions/attention-deficit-hyperactivity-disorder-adhd/

National Health Service [NHS]. (2021c, December 24). *Symptoms: Attention deficit hyperactivity disorder (ADHD)*. https://www.nhs.uk/conditions/attention-deficit-hyperactivity-disorder-adhd/symptoms/

National Institute of Neurological Disorders and Stroke [NINDS]. (2023, January 20). *Learning disabilities*. National Institute of Health. https://www.ninds.nih.gov/health-information/disorders/learning-disabilities

Neurodivergent. (2022, June 2). Cleveland Clinic. https://my.clevelandclinic.org/health/symptoms/23154-neurodivergent

Neurodiversity quotes. (n.d.). GoodReads. https://www.goodreads.com/quotes/tag/neurodiversity

Nevins, M. (2023, September 12). How to get stuff done: The Eisenhower Matrix (a.k.a. the urgent vs the important). *Forbes*. https://www.forbes.com/sites/hillennevins/2023/01/05/how-to-get-stuff-done-the-eisenhower-matrix-aka-the-urgent-vs-the-important/?sh=7490004c1b58

Office for Civil Rights. (n.d.a). *About IDEA*. IDEA - Individuals with Disabilities Education Act. https://sites.ed.gov/idea/about-idea/

Office for Civil Rights. (n.d.b). *Sec. 300.8 Child with a disability*. IDEA - Individuals with Disabilities Education Act. https://sites.ed.gov/idea/about-idea/

Office for Civil Rights (2023). *Free appropriate public education for students with disabilities: Requirements under Section 504 of the Rehabilitation Act of 1973*. https://www2.ed.gov/about/offices/list/ocr/docs/edlite-FAPE504.html

Oladipo, G. (2021, July 16). *What to know about ADHD and dopamine.* PsychCentral. https://psychcentral.com/adhd/what-to-know-about-adhd-and-dopamine

Parenting quotes. (n.d.). BrainyQuote. https://www.brainyquote.com/topics/parenting-quotes

Park, I., Gong, J., Lyons, G.L., Hirota, T., Takahashi, M., Kim, B., Lee, S., Kim, Y., Lee, J., & Leventhat, B.L. (2020). Prevalence of and factors associated with school bullying in students with Autism Spectrum Disorder: A cross-cultural meta-analysis. *Yonsei Medical Journal, 61*(11), pp. 909-922. https://doi.org/10.3349/ymj.2020.61.11.909

Pelham, W.E. & Altszuler, A. (2022, June 24). Scream-less parenting is possible with behavioral parent training. *ADDitude.* https://www.additudemag.com/behavioral-parent-training-for-adhd-adjusting-strategies/

Pesantez, N. (n.d.). Adhansia XR (discontinued). *ADDitude.* https://www.additudemag.com/medication/adhansia-xr/

Pinzone, V. De Rossi, P., Trabucchi, G., Lester, D., Girardi, P., & Pompili, M. (2019). Temperament correlates in adult ADHD: A systematic review. *Journal of Affective Disorders, 252*, pp. 394-403. https://doi.org/10.1016/j.jad.2019.04.006

Ptacek, R., Weissenberger, S., Braaten, E., Klicperova-Baker, M., Goetz, M., Raboch, J., Vnukova, M. & Stefano, G.B. (2019). Clinical implications of the perception of time in attention deficit hyperactivity disorder (ADHD): A review. *Medical Science Monitor, 25*, pp. 3918-3924. https://doi.org/10.12659/MSM.914225

Rodden, J. (2021, January 14). What is executive dysfunction? Signs and symptoms of EFD. *ADDitude.* https://www.additudemag.com/what-is-executive-function-disorder/

Rodden, J. (2023, September 5). Non-stimulant ADHD medication overview. *ADDitude.* https://www.additudemag.com/non-stimulant-adhd-medication/

Rowden, A. (2022, April 27). What causes parental anxiety and what effects does it have? *Medical News Today.* https://www.medicalnewstoday.com/articles/parental-anxiety

Rosanbalm, K.D., & Murray, D.W. (2017). *Caregiver Co-regulation Across Development: A Practice Brief.* OPRE Brief #2017-80. Washington, DC: Office of Planning, Research, and Evaluation, Administration for Children and Families, US. Department of Health and Human Services. *Frontiers in Human Neuroscience, 12.* https://doi.org/10.3389/fnhum.2018.00100

Rubia, K. (2018). Cognitive neuroscience of attention deficit hyperactivity disorder (ADHD) and its clinical translation.

Russell, L. (2023, August 13). *31 inspiring parenting quotes for hard times.* They Are The Future. https://www.theyarethefuture.co.uk/parenting-quotes-for-hard-times/

Scutti, S. (2017, February 15). *Brains of those with ADHD show smaller structures related to emotion.* CNN Health. https://edition.cnn.com/2017/02/15/health/adhd-brain-scans-study/index.html

Setyanisa, A.R., Setiawati, Y., Irwanto, I., Fithriyah, I., & Prabowo, S.A. (2022). Relationship between parenting style and risk of attention deficit hyperactivity disorder in elementary school children. *The Malaysian Journal of Medical Sciences, 29*(4), pp. 152-159. https://doi.org/10.21315/mjms2022.29.4.14

Seymour, T. (2022, October 24). Three types of ADHD: What are the differences?. *Medical News Today.* https://www.medicalnewstoday.com/articles/317815

Sibley, M.H., Swanson, J.M., Arnold, L.E., Hechtman, L.T., Owens, L.E., Stehli, A., Abikoff, H., Hinshaw, S.P., Molina, B.S.G., Mitchell, J.T., Jensen, P.S., Howard, A., Lakes, K.D., Pelham, W.E., & MTA Cooperative Group. (2017). Defining ADHD symptom persistence in adulthood: Optimizing sensitivity and specificity. *Journal of Child Psychology and Psychiatry, 58*(6), pp. 665-662. https://doi.org/10.1111/jcpp.12620

Sissons, B. (2022, August 2). What are some nonstimulant ADHD medications for adults? *Medical News Today.* https://www.medicalnewstoday.com/articles/best-nonstimulant-adhd-medication-for-adults

Sissons, B. (2023, May 30). What is executive dysfunction in ADHD? *Medical News Today.* https://www.medicalnewstoday.com/articles/adhd-executive-function

Skogli, E.W., Teicher, M.H., Andersen, P.N., Hovik, K.T., & Øie, M. (2013). ADHD in girls and boys—gender differences in co-existing symptoms and executive function measures. *BMC Psychiatry, 13*(298). https://doi.org/10.1186/1471-244X-13-298

Slobodin, O. & Davidovitch, M. (2019). Gender differences in objective and subjective measures of ADHD among clinic-referred children. *Frontiers in Human Neuroscience, 13.* https://doi.org/10.3389/fnhum.2019.00441

Soler-Gutiérrez, A.M., Pérez-González, J.C., & Mayas, J. (2023). Evidence of emotion dysregulation as a core symptom of adult ADHD: A systemic review. *PLoS One, 18*(1). https://doi.org/10.1371/journal.pone.0280131

Solution quotes. (n.d.). BrainyQuote. https://www.brainyquote.com/topics/solution-quotes

Sruthi, M. (n.d.). *What are central alpha-2 agonists and how do they work?* RxList. https://www.rxlist.com/what_are_central_alpha-2_agonists_and_how_do_they/drug-class.htm

Starkman, E. (2023, April 18). *Assistive technology for children with ADHD.* WebMD. https://www.webmd.com/add-adhd/childhood-adhd/assistive-technology-adhd

State Council on Developmental Disabilities of California [SCDD]. (n.d.). *The difference between IEPs and 504 plans.* https://scdd.ca.gov/wp-content/uploads/sites/33/2018/03/The-Difference-Between-IEP-and-504-Plans.pdf

Tee-Melegrito, R.A. (2022, October 31). How ADHD differs in males and females. *Medical News Today.*

https://www.medicalnewstoday.com/articles/is-adhd-more-common-in-males-or-females

Teixeria, M.C.T.V., Marino, R.L.D.F., Carreiro, L.R.R. (2015). Associations between inadequate parenting practices and behavioral problems in children and adolescents with attention deficit hyperactivity disorder. *The Scientific World Journal.* https://doi.org/10.1155/2015/683062

The Investopedia Team. (2022, April 7). *What is the Pareto principle—aka the Pareto rule or 80/20 rule?* Investopedia. https://www.investopedia.com/terms/p/paretoprinciple.asp

Thorell, L.B., Holst, Y., & Sjöwall, D. (2019). Quality of life in older adults with ADHD: Links to ADHD symptom levels and executive functioning deficits. *Nordic Journal of Psychiatry, 73*(7), pp. 409-416. https://doi.org/10.1080/08039488.2019.1646804

U.S. Department of Education. (n.d.). *Every Student Succeeds Act (ESSA).* https://www.ed.gov/essa?src=rn

U.S. Department of Health and Human Services (2006). *Your rights under Section 504 of the Rehabilitation Act.* https://www.hhs.gov/sites/default/files/ocr/civilrights/resources/factsheets/504.pdf

Vacher, C., Goujon, A., Romo, L., & Purper-Ouuakil, D. (2020). Efficacy of psychosocial interventions for children with ADHD and emotion dysregulation: A systematic review. *Psychiatric Research, 291.* https://doi.org/10.1016/j.psychres.2020.113151

Van Dessel, J., Sonuga-Barke, E., Moerkerke, M., Van der Oord, S., Lemiere, J., Morsink, S., & Danckaerts, M. (2018). The amygdala in adolescents with attention-deficit/hyperactivity disorder: Structural and functional correlates delay aversion. *The World Journal of Biological Psychiatry, 21*(9), pp. 673-684. https://doi.org/10.1080/15622975.2019.1585946

Van der Oord, S. & Tripp, G. (2020). How to improve behavioral parent and teacher training for children with ADHD: Integrating empirical research on learning and motivation into treatment. *Clinical Child and Family Psychology Review, 23*, pp. 577-604. https://doi.org/10.1007/s10567-020-00327-z

Villines, Z. (2021, November 30). What are the long-term effects of ADHD medication? *Medical News Today.* https://www.medicalnewstoday.com/articles/long-term-effects-of-adhd-medication

Villines, Z. (2023, June 28). How to increase dopamine with ADHD. *Medical News Today.* https://www.medicalnewstoday.com/articles/how-to-increase-dopamine-adhd

World Health Organization [WHO]. (2019). *Attention Deficit Hyperactivity Disorder (ADHD).* https://apps.who.int/iris/bitstream/handle/10665/364129/WHOEMMNH214E-eng.pdf

World Health Organization [WHO]. (2023, February 21). *Stress.* https://www.who.int/news-room/questions-and-answers/item/stress

Yellin, S. (2023, July 20). Your rights to ADHD accommodations at work. *ADDitude.* https://www.additudemag.com/adhd-law-americans-with-disabilities-act/